The Aesthetics of Self-Invention

Oscar Wilde to David Bowie

Shelton Waldrep

University of Minnesota Press
Minneapolis • London

Published by the University of Minnesota Press
111 Third Avenue South, Suite 290
Minneapolis, MN 55401-2520
http://www.upress.umn.edu

Library of Congress Cataloging-in-Publication Data

Waldrep, Shelton.
  The aesthetics of self-invention : Oscar Wilde to David Bowie / Shelton Waldrep.
    p. cm.
  Includes bibliographical references and index.
  ISBN 0-8166-3417-3 (hc : alk. paper) — ISBN 0-8166-3418-1 (pb : alk. paper)
  1. Wilde, Oscar, 1854–1900—Aesthetics. 2. Wilde, Oscar, 1854–1900—Knowledge—
Performing arts. 3. Modernism (Literature)—Great Britain. 4. Aesthetics, British—19th century.
5. Aesthetics, Modern—20th century. 6. Performing arts—Great Britain. 7. Romanticism—
Great Britain. 8. Bowie, David. I. Title.
  PR5827.A35W35 2004
  828′.809—dc22
                                                      2004006606

Printed in the United States of America on acid-free paper

The University of Minnesota is an equal-opportunity educator and employer.

12 11 10 09 08 07 06 05 04   10 9 8 7 6 5 4 3 2 1

For Jane and Chloe

Contents

Acknowledgments

Work on this project spanned a great deal of time and overlapped with major events in my life—the death of my dissertation adviser, Clyde de L. Ryals, who was a *Doktorvater* in the best possible sense; the death of my beloved mother, Nina Smith Waldrep; and the birth of my beautiful daughter, Chloe Nina Waldrep. While it is not possible for me to express how the past years have been both the best and the worst of times, without the support of family and friends they would have been too much to bear. I especially thank my sister, Rosa Lee Waldrep, and my father, Floyd Waldrep.

This book came out of a rich experience as a graduate student at Duke University, and I would like to thank many people there whose guidance and assistance made my work possible. Most especially, the members of my examination and dissertation committees (Susan Willis, Fredric Jameson, Jane M. Gaines, Eve Kosofsky Sedgwick, Michael Moon, Kenneth Surin), as well as members of the faculty who provided key support along the way (Van Hillard, Marianna Torgovnick). They deserve the credit that the historical moment that was the Duke English department in the late eighties and early nineties is due.

I would like to acknowledge the opportunity to deliver portions of this work at various events (conferences, job talks, invited presentations) held at the University of Southern Maine, University of California–Davis, Northwestern University, Bates College, Colby College, Dartmouth College, Hofstra University, the Dead Space Gallery in Portland, Maine, and Georgia State University. I am grateful to the hosts who sponsored me at these places. At the University of Southern Maine, Melanie Beaudette and Dominique Bartels relieved me of the burden of the index and deserve special note for their professionalism and unflappability. Finally, I express my warmest regards for my editors at the University of Minnesota Press, especially Richard W. Morrison, whose patience and amiability made the process of publication so nearly painless, and to the anonymous readers of the manuscript, who were both helpful and generous.

Positioning Wilde before and after Modernism

In a sense, a study of Oscar Wilde begins with the invention of Wilde as we know him; namely, the self-designated "professor of aesthetics," as he identified himself on his visiting cards when he came down from Oxford to London in 1879. It is at this time that Wilde embarked on his first great period in which he not only reinvented himself yet again but also had to earn money and make his way in the commercial world. Wilde's transformation at this point in his life was certainly not his first—nor his last—but marks the most significant in his career, as Wilde made clear that he saw his identity as something mutable. For anyone who was interested, he was making the claim that he could—he had—redesigned not just his image but himself. Wilde's subsequent trajectory was not toward some ultimate being—some essential or irreducible self—but the beginning in earnest of a system of becoming, of transformations of self that left any belief that there could be a natural, stable Oscar Wilde in doubt.

Wilde's legacy as both a writer and a literary figure of social, political, and cultural significance is such that Wilde the man cannot be readily separated from Wilde the careerist. His roles as aesthete, lecturer, businessman, family man, poet, editor, playwright, seducer, prisoner, and exile are part of a broader role of writer as performer that he used self-consciously in an attempt to destroy the binary opposition separating art and life. Beginning at least as early as his career at Oxford,

Wilde was captivated by the idea that one could make one's life artis-tic—a concept that would have been familiar to him in his education in the classics. Wilde's other interests at this time were in philosophies and belief systems that tended to emphasize the physical world. That is, Wilde's Oxford notebooks—with their references to Hegel and Pater— also included an attempt to combine historicizing aesthetic systems with the empirical work of Spencer and Darwin. Though keeping such notebooks was common, as Linda Dowling notes, "Wilde's notations are unusual, however, in the way they continually strive to translate the conceptual language of one author or thinker into the intellectual system of another. . . . Here we see commencing in rough outline the process that would culminate in *Decay of Lying* and *Critic as Artist* . . . which would later have such far-reaching consequences for twentieth-century literature and criticism."[1] Wilde's attempts to disrupt the com-placency of his time were not merely replays of the earlier ideas of others; rather, he was intent on joining what he would soon label a renaissance in the arts in England to an exploration of the real, mate-rial world around him. Wilde was interested in decoration not only as something beautiful as form, for example, but also as something useful as function. In fact, it was not by chance that his earliest polemical writ-ing is on decoration and various concepts of style—whether in women's clothing or in room decor—because it was the utilitarian aspects of these products, the bridge they represented between the physical and the ideal, that fascinated him.[2]

Wilde's belief in transcendence through the beauty of things was actually tied to an almost Platonic belief in which the register of the beauty in heaven is the beauty on Earth. Unlike Plato, Wilde seemed quite content to celebrate this earthly beauty for its own sake. Yet his emphasis on surfaces, his belief in the visible as opposed to the invisible world,[3] shows that his various proclamations to dismiss realism are at least a red herring—if not simply part of another argument altogether. Wilde's interest in the real world—including both its injustices and ugly aspects—is proved time and again not only by the inclusion of what Pater termed "realism" in the Jim Vane portions of *The Picture of Dorian*

Gray (1891) but also in Wilde's references to and descriptions of emotions, characters, and facts from various trades and class strata that occur consistently throughout his oeuvre. Wilde's passion for the real is, in fact, consistent with his desire to transform life into art: only someone who knows life well could ever want to change it into something else.

Wilde's system of transformation was not a simple one and appears to many critics to have taken material form only when Wilde began either to lead a double life or to act on his "latent" tendencies—in either case, exaggerating behaviors that ultimately led to his end. Only in the past several years, with work coming out of queer theory by Eve Kosofsky Sedgwick, Lee Edelman, Richard Dellamora, Wayne Koestenbaum, and Neil Bartlett, has one been able to posit another explanation for the course Wilde's career followed and the relationship it might have had to his personal life.[4] Other critics have—perhaps unwittingly—supported the work of these various queer theorists by problematizing the relationship Wilde had to the thought of his age. That is, they have begun to remap the influences on Wilde as they might have come from his readings as a student at Oxford (Smith and Helfand), his relationship to the construction of authority and professionalism of his time (Ian Small), or even the relationship between Wilde and his public (John Stokes, Regenia Gagnier, Rachel Bowlby). The portrait that results from combining the work of both streams of criticism is to see that the definition that we have of Wilde—our current general assessment of his work—is not only in flux but in need of radical rethinking and a comprehensive reformulation. As Bartlett asks, "Who was that man?"

In response to Bartlett, I would say Wilde was a romantic whose concept of romantic individuality was an extension of the ideas of the University of Jena school of philosophers, Friedrich Schlegel paramount among them.[5] Wilde did not see the ultimate end of individualism as having a certifiable telos. Rather, he treated the newly forming concept of personality ironically. His personality and philosophy, one could say, were one and the same, and the best definition that one may have of either is that Wilde's concept of self was similar to Schlegel's concept of philosophy. As Clyde de L. Ryals says of romantic irony: "Its purpose is not to persuade, amuse, or ridicule but, rather, to question certainties and present possibilities. It is essentially philosophical and is a response to the problem of contradictions in life that are perceived as irreconcilable."[6] Indeed, Wilde's genius may well have been his ability to understand that which cannot be reconciled. His use of paradox and irony in much of his prose and nearly all of his aphorisms is a structural clue to this. His personal transformations, therefore, far from being only about uncertainty or marketability, were an embodiment of a tradition of Continental thought—by then several decades old, but by no means fully understood.

A primary precursor for Wilde, therefore, may have been a particular strain of German romanticism that he was to embrace via the formulation of the dandy—a concept and performance begun by Byron and perfected by Disraeli—which Wilde was ultimately to transform, first into "aestheticism" and later, with the help of the French, into "decadence." Though this timeline is, to some extent, the usual one applied to Wilde and his relationship to the intellectual periods of his age, I would like to argue that it is the beginning and end of Wilde's life that we understand the least and which we should turn to if a new understanding of him is to be gained. That is, how did Wilde transform romanticism into something else? And similarly, what was the final phase of Wilde's influence?

Most critics would probably place Wilde's telos in modernism. Isobel Murray, for instance, notes that "irony is a key term in Modernist approaches to literature: perhaps Wilde has more in common with some of the 'Great Modernists' than has hitherto been allowed."[7] Indeed, there are connections between romanticism and modernism that are fairly obvious, and for some time now sympathetic critics of Wilde's work have often seen it as a primary precursor to modernism.[8] How Wilde may actually have influenced modernist writers, however, is much more difficult to place. One has Yeats's own paean to Wilde in his *Autobiographies*, but it is not clear what connections there may be between Wilde and many other writers in the modernist period. It may be that Wilde's reputation flourished most noticeably in the period after modernism and that the place to look for his legacy is in postmodern performative structures. Toward this end, an important reevaluation of Wilde may be Koestenbaum's essay "Wilde's Hard Labor and the Birth of Gay Reading," which begins to investigate the way in which Wilde self-consciously redesigned himself during and after his imprisonment as a type for a new generation of readers.[9] Koestenbaum illustrates the many ways in which the typing of "Wilde"—both literally and figuratively—meant the same as typing "homosexual," a concept that became more conveniently available after Wilde's "exposure." Koestenbaum rereads Wilde's postprison literature—and his interest in the design of the book editions published after his release—for evidence that he not only accepted his typing but attempted to ensure its dissemination into the next century through the books he would leave behind. In other words, Wilde understood the identity he had been given and not only accepted it but embraced it, though he wished to define it in his own way. During and after prison, Wilde began to construct his last self-conscious identity for himself—in this case, one that was the precursor to what would be thought of as "homosexual" after his death.

To rethink Wilde's contribution to our century's thought, therefore, it is necessary to see how Wilde saw himself and the extent to which—even now—the intellectual contribution that he was to offer has never been adequately understood. Although Terry Eagleton, Gagnier, and others have gone a long way toward helping us to decipher the influences on Wilde's thinking, I would like to track the influence that Wilde was to have on postmodernism by looking at certain strains and tropes in his writing and performance that reappear only to be codified—made into a type—to be replayed in variations in the next century in the work of Truman Capote, Andy Warhol, and David Bowie. The typing of Wilde, indeed, is made up of a concentration of the influences that he succumbed to and to elements original with him—especially his own interest in materialism and, specifically, something like a queer identity.

Why Wilde may be more of a major figure now than in, say, the first half of the twentieth century has much to do with the reevaluation of him made possible in a post-Stonewall era and the availability of poststructuralist tools with which to evaluate and describe the effects on language that, in his aphoristic and ironic treatment of it, are left deconstructed. Roughly paralleling these interpretive breakthroughs were changes in post–World War II culture brought about by the growth of the media and the hypercommercialization of art and literature— changes that allowed for the erosion of the difference between artist and promoter, writer and star, to seem much more common than before. Indeed, by the 1980s—the period that Steven M. L. Aronson, for one, calls the age of hype—Wilde's eccentricity seems almost mild, as the excesses of our own fin de siècle seem much more portentous, if less potentially generative than his.[10]

"The dandy as dialectical materialist,"[11] as Eagleton terms it, is a version of Wilde that is perhaps best known in non-Anglophone countries, where Wilde's best-selling book has always been *The Soul of Man* (1891).[12] But the idea that the theoretical underpinnings of both his work and his persona are based on a socialist agenda is not often noted in the works on Wilde until recently. In fact, the specter of Wilde all but haunts Eagleton's discussion in *The Ideology of the Aesthetic* of the trope of the body and its importance to Nietzsche, Marx, and Freud. As Eagleton proclaims, "Aesthetics is born as a discourse of the body."[13] This argument reflects a broad spectrum of beliefs within gender studies that—contrary to many poststructuralist positions—have in common a desire to be aware of the actual, concrete forces that act on one's body while at the same time attempting to avoid the construction of an essentialist discourse around it.

As Sedgwick points out in her *Epistemology of the Closet*, modernist authors such as Nietzsche and Freud were obsessed with the body and their relationship to it, while Eagleton and Gagnier go so far as to claim Marx as an aesthete.[14] Yet the boundary between materialism and aesthetics may well be a tenuous one. Wilde wrote *The Soul of Man*, after all, during the same period that he wrote *Dorian Gray*. Indeed, as Eagleton notes: "If he [Wilde] sometimes has the offensive irresponsibility of the aesthete, he also restores to us something of the full political force of that term, as a radical rejection of mean-spirited utility and a devotion to human self-realization as an end in itself which is very close to the writings of Karl Marx."[15] Much of what we assume to be Wilde's ploy for idleness and the upending of Victorian bourgeois platitudes can also be seen as an attempt to break from the bonds that held him.[16] Gagnier observes this impulse in Wilde's attack on the press in *The Soul of Man* and in his ability to display "acute social criticism" of the middle and upper classes from his early work through *The Importance of Being Earnest*.[17] Gagnier takes this argument even further to claim that "Wilde's argument in 'The Soul of Man' is clearly within the mainstream tradition of socialist thought (if not practice), but less recognized in its consistency with a long tradition of socialist aesthetics."[18] She cites Schiller's *Letters on the Aesthetic Education of Man* (1795), Marx and Engels in *The German Ideology* (1846), Morris in his "How We Live and How We Might Live" (1884), Trotsky in his conclusion to *Literature and Revolution* (1924), and Marcuse in "Some Social Implications of Modern Technology" (1941),[19] which brings Wilde's materialism up to the period that I trace to him and shows his continuity with a specifically socialist tradition. If the "problem" of the body is common to the seminal thinkers of the past two centuries, then certainly Wilde's own ideas—though less dogmatically systematic and influential—can still be seen as an attempt at an answer to the same questions. In fact, the bringing together of the lived and the aesthetic—the seen and the unseen—is exactly what Wilde attempted in his work. Wilde's aestheticism, therefore, is not just an escape from commercialism or the tyranny of the middle class but also an attempt at rewriting aesthetics by working through the body from a materialist standpoint.[20] Wilde's ultimate lesson was to be found in prison, when control over his own body was taken away and he was able to see all too well just what injustice and the suffering of the body were about.

Part I of this book argues that self-invention is a discursive, literary, rhetorical, and commodity concern for Wilde that is paradigmatic of the transformations his writing, career, and public and private lives were to take. Wilde's fashioning of a complex system of personae was fueled by an erotics of opportunity—a desire to become socially respectable, professionally serious, and to have both a marriage and an existence in the demimonde of London. Guiding this urban mythos—which still exists, in ways unchanged, in London today—was a critical and creative impulse that is apparent not only in his writing but in his choices in life as well. Linking these concepts within Wilde's philosophy was his ability to restate the basic concepts of German romanticism as an "English renaissance of the arts" or as a "return to romance." Wilde's queer—or, perhaps more accurately, bisexual—identity is integral to the larger program he had of releasing people from any sort of bonds that might hold them. This materialist belief, therefore, was linked to a type of queer socialism much like that which Edward Carpenter would perfect in the next century.[21] Wilde's version, however, was ultimately quite different. Whereas Carpenter emphasized fraternity and ruggedness of a sort that might remind one of the homosocial impulses of Teddy Roosevelt, Wilde attempted to design a system that freed one's talents for individuality and considered charity of any sort as one of the greatest indicators of oppression. That is, Wilde saw what he called "individualism" as the greatest good within society because it is a "disintegrating force" that breaks up "monotony of type" and frees individuals to develop their full potential.[22] Private property hampers individualism by confusing the person with what he or she owns. Socialism is preferable to other forms of government, therefore, because it breaks the individual's bonds both to property and to other people. In his emphasis on self-development and, by implication, the role that sexuality seems to play in it, Wilde's approach is similar to that theorized by Michel Foucault in his work on sexuality and Greek culture.

In an interview from 1984, Foucault described the project of the second and third volumes of *The History of Sexuality* as one concerned with "an *art of existence*, or rather let's say a *technique of life*. It was a matter of knowing how to govern one's own life in order to give it the most beautiful form possible. . . . That's what I tried to reconstitute: the formation and development of a practice of self whose objective was to constitute oneself as the worker of the beauty of one's own life."[23] For

Foucault, the ancient Greek idea of life as a work of art was a moral concept—one later replaced, in Christianity, with church doxa. One of the many differences between the two systems was the fact that the care of the self was concerned with "personal liberty," while "the religion of the text" produced "a code of rules."[24] This change did not mean that Foucault felt the Greeks were particularly worthy of praise. He labels their search for a stylish existence "obstinate" and their attempt to find a way to make it common to everyone a misguided mistake.[25] While Wilde held a much higher view of the Greek system, he and Foucault both saw the Greeks in relation to the Christian era that followed them. For Foucault, ancient Greece did not problematize the notion of the self—a written self—in the way that Christianity did via diaries and "a spiritual movement linking individual experiences . . . which allowed it to judge or in any case to appraise the reactions of each person."[26] Foucault's *History of Sexuality* links to his work on the Greeks in the first volume, which posits the late-nineteenth-century emergence of homosexuality as a category of the individual (rather than an activity) to the rise of the personal confession in religion and the law. As Foucault notes, by giving "the one who listened" the power to interpret the confession—to make the confession a text to be understood—"the nineteenth century gave itself the possibility of causing the procedures of confession to operate within the regular formation of a scientific discourse."[27] The result of this invention was to "put into operation an entire machinery for producing true discourses concerning it. Not only did it speak of sex and compel everyone to do so; it also set out to formulate the uniform truth of sex."[28] One result was "the formation of a 'reverse' discourse: homosexuality began to speak in its own behalf, to demand that its legitimacy or 'naturality' be acknowledged."[29]

Wilde's own generative system of discourse was not so much about homosexuality—and its inevitable birth—as about the Attic Greek idea of liberty for the individual. As Gagnier, echoing Jonathan Dollimore, theorizes, "Foucault's 'aesthetics of the self' ought to be interpreted not as a technology of the self but as an alternative to it, as a way that sexual practices or 'pleasures' might enable other selves and new relationships to emerge."[30] While she acknowledges that this image of sexuality might seem "idealist and masculine in its freedom and self-control,"[31] it is a vision that seems closest to Wilde's own. Though Wilde is obviously immensely important as a gay icon, as Michael Doylen argues:

> Foucault's "homosexual *askêsis*" names a technology of self-stylization whereby gay men and lesbians might eventually move beyond the limiting view of sexuality as containing the truth of the self. His formulation involves a fundamental irony: the social marginalization of homosexuals as essentially "reverse" may motivate those individuals to invent self-identifications and social relationships that problematize and undo essentialist notions of the sexual self.[32]

Wilde's influence beyond his death was in codifying his ideas as a network of writerly and performative characteristics. Part II of this book takes up the specific arrangement of these characteristics, as well as their deployment by him and other figures in our century, as they form a unique configuration that may be identified as "avant-garde," "postmodern," or "queer" but is ultimately uniquely Wilde's. Although the birth of Wilde's influence may have been a part of the tradition we now call modernism—especially in its originary state—it is in the contemporary, post–World War II era that the Wildean paradigm takes root and becomes significant. This book attempts to trace the Wildean trope as it registers in the century Wilde was never to see. His influence—as homosexual "other"—was to affect the twentieth century in profound ways both as a source of queer influence and as a model for postmodern performance, literary and otherwise.

Carried on into the twentieth century, Wilde's skills at self-promotion perhaps reach their apex in Capote's and Bowie's abilities to use television, film, and video, hence combining sound with visuals and the weird intimacy that television seems to suggest—perhaps especially in its ability to showcase a "personality." Quite possibly, Wilde foresaw much of this in his own *Salomé*, a play banned in England during his lifetime. Designed as a vehicle for the specific personality of

Sarah Bernhardt, the play was meant to showcase her stardom and voice. With its rococo sexual situations, stylized language, elaborate sets, and costumes that emphasized the visual as antirealist spectacle—not to mention its Oriental subject matter, gay characters, and general drag atmosphere—Wilde composed a drama as rock concert.[33] Or rather, Bowie finally staged Wilde's play in England and elsewhere over and over again as the key to understanding a new type of cultural difference that Wilde had discovered a century before.

PART I

CHAPTER 1

Wilde's Romantic Irony

Facing the Dialectic

> The nineteenth-century dislike of realism is the rage of Caliban seeing his own face in the glass.
>
> The nineteenth-century dislike of romanticism is the rage of Caliban not seeing his own face in the glass.
>
> —Wilde, in his preface to *The Picture of Dorian Gray*

In writing about Hegel's dialects, Terry Eagleton describes Hegel's theory as an "infinity of endless self-reflection" in which

> the aesthetic represents a break with sensuous immediacy . . . a lapse into abyssal specularity . . . with no more resolute centering of the subject than can be found in the "imaginary" of bodily immediacy. Hamlet and Caliban are thus inverted mirror-images of each other; one is always in the aesthetic, either too much or too little oneself, ensnared in actuality or adrift in possibility, lacking that dialectical tension between these realms which is defined by the ethical paradox of becoming what one is.[1]

This formulation neatly illustrates the version of Hegel that appears to have been so attractive to Wilde.[2] That is, Wilde saw the dialectical process as acting both on the individual and his age, with realism and romanticism existing in a dialectical relationship with each other.[3] Indeed, in various writings, Wilde calls for the return of either "romance," as he does in "The Portrait of Mr. W. H." and "The Critic as Artist,"[4] or a romantic movement as a new school distinct from realism. Although realism was considered by many at the time to be the movement that most deserved the distinction of being new—especially when reconstituted as naturalism—Wilde's own sense was that naturalism had already had its day. His idea of what constituted this new romantic movement, however, was a changeable one. As early as his North American tour, he saw romanticism as equivalent to the English Renaissance that he espoused, but by the time of "The Critic as Artist," romanticism had become the code word for his own critical and creative doctrines.

Although romanticism was a new movement to Wilde, it came, paradoxically, from the past. Wilde was careful to explain, however, what it was that he wanted to recover and, more specifically, how his entire return to romance was a dialectical move. That is, there had always been swings from some form of classicism to some form of medievalism; therefore if the age was realistic (in more than just literature), then the next phase must be romantic. This dialectical configuration becomes complicated when one attempts to map it onto what Wilde means by the "classical" (or "Hellenic" or "Greek") and the "medieval." The two dialectical systems do not actually line up; rather, they cross, overlap, and subdivide according to the context of Wilde's discussion and the particular point he is trying to make.[5] The task of tracing Wilde's changing meanings for these pairs of concepts is made even more difficult by the fact that he often shifts registers—even in midsentence—in many of his critical writings.[6] However, the primary significance in Wilde's use of a concept of "romanticism" may be in the implications that this term has for the numerous aspects of this tradition with which Wilde aligned himself. In his review of Pater's *Appreciations* (1898), for example, Wilde argued that "to realise the nineteenth century, one must realise every century that has preceded it, and that has contributed to its making." Indeed, Wilde goes on to say, "To know anything about oneself, one must know all about others. There must be no mood with which one cannot sympathise, no dead mode of life that one cannot make alive."[7] Wilde's acceptance of the past as the key to the present is not only a decadent pitch for new experiences but also an indication of his willingness to learn from the past, to absorb from previous periods and movements. His privileging of the concept of romanticism, with the antiqueness that this phrase might conjure, was an attempt by him to signal not only his dialectical relationship to realism but also that romanticism was a concept rich in connotation for the present.[8]

As with many of his key terms, there is a good chance that Wilde was referencing the conceptual vocabulary of Pater, whose postscript to *Appreciations* was originally entitled "Romanticism" when it was first published in *Macmillan's Magazine* (November 1876). In this piece Pater discusses romanticism as a specific tradition "within the last hundred years" in Germany and France—represented by Tieck and Goethe in the former and Gautier in the latter. He defines the term as one that need not be

> a limited application to the manifestation of those qualities at a particular period. But the romantic spirit is, in reality, an ever-present, an enduring principle, in the artistic temperament; and the qualities of thought and style which that, and other similar uses of the word *romantic* really indicate, are indeed but symptoms of a very continuous and widely working influence.[9]

Pater concludes that although romanticism and classicism have specific meanings for the present, they are still "but one variation of an old opposition, which may be traced from the very beginning of the formation of European art and literature."[10] Or as he says later in the essay, "To turn always with that ever-changing spirit, yet to retain the flavour of what was admirably done in past generations, in the classics, as we say—is the problem of true romanticism."[11]

Pater's theory of romanticism could also be a description of Wilde's dual use of the term as a label for both a general critical movement and a recent historical period. Pater suggests that the romantic not only is

a part of a dialectic but also constitutes a tradition—or a problematic—
that each generation of European artists must face.[12] As Pater implies,
romanticism may well be a mode or form of avant-garde critical self-
consciousness as much as a "temporally circumscribed phenomenon." In
this sense especially, Wilde's inheritance and championing of a romantic tradition is at least as much an engagement in a certain type of
romantic praxis as it is the taking on of the mantle of a particular
school. In searching for the meaning of romanticism for Wilde, therefore, the most likely candidates are the ones that would come closest to
this self-critical style. Hence Pater's identification of Gautier—often
thought of as a protodecadent—is one strain, while his identification of
the German romantics is yet another. In looking at the particular kind
of formal and critical work being done by Wilde in his criticism and
in his performance as a critic and writer—and taking into account the
ways in which his career evolved from poetry to criticism to the novel
to drama—his most potent and immediately discernible critical model
for romanticism seems to be not so much French decadence as German
romanticism. For while Gautier's *l'art pour l'art* is obviously a part of
Wilde's doctrine, if taken as a whole, his career seems much closer to the
form of the modern avant-garde of Friedrich Schlegel.[13]

In his study of the literary heritage of the Athenaeum group,
Eric A. Blackall notes that it is to Schlegel that one must turn to get at
the core of the circle's philosophy and aesthetics.[14] In his approach to
both the novel and the fragment—indeed, in his choice of these forms
over others—Schlegel showed a desire to break down barriers by re-
examining the literary forms and artistic theories of the day. In placing
irony at the center of these reexaminations, he created a movement based
on instability and protomodernist experimentation of which Wilde is
both the heir and the greatest exemplar. As Julia Prewitt Brown argues,
"Wilde's vision of the new artist-critic displays an ambition to overcome the opposition between abstract and concrete, criticism and creation . . . an ambition akin to that of the early Romantics in Germany."[15]
Even if Wilde would not claim Schlegel as a major influence, placing
Wilde within the lineage of German romanticism highlights the scope

of Wilde's possible models for future writers and practitioners of self-performance. Specifically, Wilde's belief in the importance of the spoken word (both the dialogue and aphoristic fragment), the mixing of genre and media, and the centrality of the recurring idea of the mask—especially in its relationship to reinvention of the self—are key to understanding Wilde's influence in the twentieth century and beyond.

In his desire to make philosophy ironic and irony philosophic, Schlegel combined theory with practice and metaphysics with aesthetics.[16] Interested in the play of the inside with the outside, he saw the artist as a hovering presence that flits between the work and the *hors-texte*. For Schlegel, this hovering, or parabasis, is of necessity anti-mimetic. Works of art, as well as philosophies, are always becoming, not being, and are always performances or actions.[17] In his unfinished novel *Lucinde* and in his philosophical fragments, Schlegel is always both controlling and mocking, representing and presenting, chaotic and static, though the latter always gives way to a new chaos that realigns into a new stasis that gives way again in a never-ending ontological pattern. For Schlegel, then, irony is a potent, all-inclusive concept for a mode of life, a practice of thought, and a type of art. Intersubjectivity—the communication (action) between subjects (other ironists)—is one of Schlegel's supreme goals, though he does see irony as having a social good in that it is a self-transcending, knowledge-giving, and ultimately positive action.

Wilde's own version of irony was part of the same destabilizing, antiteleological strain that surfaces in Schlegel's theory. The "attitude of anarchistic defiance" that can be located in Wilde and the decadent movement is part of an entire pattern of romantic resistance to both bourgeois culture and rationalism.[18] However, "Romanticism, with its fury of frenzied action," as Mario Praz calls it, was supposed to contrast to "decadence, with its sterile contemplation," though "the subject-matter is almost the same."[19] Indeed, though romanticism as a movement in the nineteenth century is often associated with a figure such as the artist Delacroix, it was, in the hands of the Jena school, a very different strain, in many ways much closer to a form of proto-aestheticism.

Like Baudelaire, Schlegel and Wilde expressed these qualities not only in the ways in which they performed their roles as writers and artists but in their work as well. The structural similarities between Wilde's dialogues, plays, fiction, poems in prose, and critical writing generally and Schlegel's unfinished novel and critical fragments suggest that Wilde's inheritance from Schlegel not only was significant but essentially restated Schlegel's and his circle's beliefs, though with changes made to reflect Wilde's dawning interests in sexuality and social protest. For both men, the ideal form for art would be one that allowed the artist to combine art with life. This ultimate form of subjectivity would, in their minds, engender the most objective structure, as it would be the most heterogeneous. In his early writings, Schlegel conceived of the dialogue as serving this purpose, but his later work shifted toward the novel. Similarly for Wilde, "The Decay of Lying" was an attempt at forging a new form of criticism that was, in a sense, soon usurped by *Dorian Gray* and then, ultimately, the experimental farce of *The Importance of Being Earnest*, arguably the logical conclusion to Schlegel's romantic irony.[20] As Eagleton notes, Wilde's irony is not the irony of "endless self-reflection,"[21] in which the "aesthete-ironist" "flamboyantly refashions the whole of its finite being in the image of its arbitrary desire."[22] Though Kierkegaard's Socrates might be an appropriate model for this type of being, Wilde's own irony demonstrates that commitment does not necessarily negate irony, but "raises the ambivalence of irony to a higher level, preserving something of its sceptical stance towards social reality but combining it with positive belief. To that extent, irony is sublated to humour and comedy, which in debunking the world's pretensions carry with them a deeper positivity than Socratic subversion."[23]

The combining of the form of the critical dialogue with that of fiction can be seen in the sudden intrusion of playlets in Schlegel's *Lucinde*, which not only shatter the realist effect on which novels usually depend but also emphasize the innate artificiality of art by using theatricality as an antirealist metaphor.[24] In breaking with mimesis, Schlegel is invoking the novel's potential role as a critical form.[25] The specific version of this form is the Socratic tradition—especially its overt pedagogic function.

Perhaps most striking in this respect are the ways in which for Wilde the dialogic form does not really connote a conversation—the element needed if the form is to function at all as a fiction. That is, Wilde's Socratic dialogues, unlike Schlegel's, are not really exchanges of dialogue at all. Though "The Critic as Artist," for instance, has two "acts" that are interrupted by the characters going down to "supper," the dialogue, like that of "The Decay of Lying," consists of one character who is the monologist and another character who is there to listen.[26] This use of the critical dialogic form disrupts the traditional format, which is, as Patricia Flanagan Behrendt observes, one in which

> the elder Socrates questions the younger disciple, thereby guiding him to a greater level of perception and self-knowledge. Plato's Socrates, who often remarks upon his own attraction to the beautiful youths with whom he converses . . . draws the young men to him through the particular dynamic of his conversational style. Since Socrates is the respected sage, the young men are attracted to him because they are flattered by his probing questions and by his attentive concern with their answers.[27]

In "The Decay of Lying," however, the younger member of the tandem is mainly there to give information, not have it elicited from him.[28] Though the questions still come from the older speaker, they are no longer "designed logically to draw thoughts from the auditor."[29] Wilde, in other words, subverts the form from a model of seduction by attention to one of seduction—and knowledge—arrived at through performance.

It is via the epigram—the self-contained turn of phrase—that performance is most obviously encoded as dialogue in Wilde, just as in Pater it is via the Heraclitian fragment. Wilde would have agreed with Schlegel when he wrote that "a fragment, like a miniature work of art, has to be entirely isolated from the surrounding world and be complete in itself."[30] However, although a fragment seems independent, it depends, like a dramatic form, on an audience for its completion. Wilde, keenly aware of the need for younger listeners in the critical dialogues, has Dorian himself "poisoned" by the "strange new philosophy" that enters through his ears. Indeed, that aphoristic dialogue might have an actual effect on the young is amply illustrated by Wilde's publication of "Phrases and Philosophies for the Use of the Young" in the first issue of *The Chameleon*: the same publication that was to come back and haunt him at the trials where the aphorism's ability to act as a form of flirtation was made a material part of the case against him.

To claim the aphoristic structure as art not only was a polemical argument for giving the form prominence but also mirrored a conceit held by Schlegel and actually practiced by Wilde: that the fragment could be the perfect hybrid art form, the one form that could contain all the others. A central doctrine of German romanticism was that "since no one literary genre can accommodate this fusion [of art, science, and poetry], all genres are therefore to be combined." Romantic irony must take "all forms, modes, styles, and genres for its expression, it will employ, *inter alia*, fragments, differing perspectives, critical comments, disruptions of cause and effect, and confessional interpolations."[31] With its elliptical, self-contained structure and ability to siphon the technical effects of various genres and discourses, it is naturally a perfect example of Schlegel's desire for *Universalpoesie*.[32] The fragment is able to unify all discourses—to become a multigeneric form—while at the same time acting as the vehicle for personality, as a fictional marker for the creation of a self. Clyde Ryals, quoting Schlegel, notes that for the ironic artist, "*Universalpoesie* is a 'form . . . fit for expressing the entire spirit of the author' and [is] why 'many artists who started to write only a novel ended up by providing us with a portrait of themselves.'"[33] The epigram not only requires an artist but creates a subject position: an artist who would use this form to create, and thus reveal, himself.[34]

In his *Die Enzyklopädie*, Novalis created a plan for a philosophical work that would be written as a series of fragments and attempt to carry out a central idea of the Athenaeum collective—namely, that its members would attempt to resynthesize knowledge to create a new poetic form. The use of the encyclopedia as the model points to the fact that the Jena group did not shy away from reflecting the real world. Indeed, as Schlegel says, "Idealism in any form must transcend itself in one way or another, in order to be able to return to itself and remain what it is. Therefore there must and will arise from the matrix of idealism a new and equally infinite realism."[35] To some extent, encyclopedia, novel, and poem were interchangeable concepts. The *Bildung*, for instance, was simply an encyclopedia "of the intellectual life of an outstanding individual."[36] The novel as a form allowed for the inclusion of various genres and, like an encyclopedia, allowed for a compendium of information, forms, and discourses. The ultimate result for this heterogeneity, however, was not a new form of objective cataloging, like an actual encyclopedia, but a new form of subjectivity. The novel as conceived by Schlegel was confessional and autobiographical. It was, in other words, a series of long fragments.

Though the fragment is potentially the form of the future for Schlegel and Wilde, both writers attempted to combine their fragments in the longer form of a novel, the principal genre of the day. Schlegel calls "novels . . . the Socratic dialogues of our time. And this free form has become the refuge of common sense in its flight from pedantry."[37] Wilde's own contribution to this genre would echo Schlegel's and become part of the tradition of romantic irony that Wilde ultimately redefined.[38]

A Garland of Fragments: *The Picture of Dorian Gray*

> Arabesques . . . together with confessions . . . are the only romantic products of nature in our age.
>
> —Schlegel

> One should never listen. To listen is a sign of indifference to one's hearers.
>
> —Wilde

Although numerous books and stories have been credited as the antecedents to Wilde's novel, it is fairly certain that one of the primary models was Disraeli's *Vivian Grey* (1826). Not only does Wilde's title provide an homage, but Disraeli was always one of Wilde's favorite authors. Indeed, Disraeli's silver-fork novel not only provides one of the Ur-types of the fictional dandy but was written during the period when German romanticism was in vogue. Stanley Weintraub argues that in the second part of the book, German romanticism provides the "glue to hold together his [Disraeli's] caricatures of contemporaries and their witty talk."[39] Weintraub conjectures that Wilde read the copy of *Vivian Grey* in his mother's library and probably got the idea for *Dorian Gray* there.[40] Though Wilde's parallels with Schlegel are key to understanding the philosophy that links his life to his work via the performance of a writerly persona, Disraeli is a more recent and powerful example and may have provided Wilde with not only a version of the English dandy but the structure of the German romantic novel as well.[41]

Schlegel traced the origins of the modern novel to the prose romance, which he likened to a series of short novels. In fact, Schlegel attempted to stretch the meaning of the word "romance" (as in the German word *Roman*) to include not only most novels but also other genres, including poetry.[42] Schlegel hoped to transform the novel into a new total artwork—a multi- or transgeneric structure that would allow literary genres to exist side by side and provide the author with a latitude similar to what can be found in a play or dialogue.[43] In other words, Schlegel believed that the novel could be the long form of the fragment—the logical extension of the logic of the fragment. The same qualities that are inherent in the fragment or epigram are expanded and multiplied in the novel form. As Anne K. Mellor contends, the novel as defined by Schlegel

> is . . . an arbitrary mixture . . . of all known literary genres: poetry, song, prose, dramatic exchanges, epic, pastoral, satire, mock-heroic, and so on. As such, Schlegel's concept of the novel is fundamentally opposed to the "great tradition" of the English novel . . . a tradition that demands a unified and logical structure, an overt yet subtle moral stance, and a concern with the realizable possibilities of life; a tradition that dismisses the novels of Sterne. . . . Instead, the genre of romantic irony is much closer

to . . . a form that combines prose, dialogue, and verse in an elaborate dis-section and playing off, one against another, of varying mental attitudes.[44]

In fact, *Lucinde* contains sections that advertise their generic form: "An Idyll of Idleness" and "Allegory of Impudence," for example, and he had plans to add verse sections as well. As one of the most versatile writers of his day in terms of the variety of forms he attempted and mixed together, Wilde shared a similar interest in stretching the possibilities of generic form. One aspect of Wilde's own interests was the way in which literature could mirror the static qualities of painting or the abstract qualities of music. Certainly a desire to represent visual expe-riences in words is an important part of the decadent tradition that Wilde inherited. Though Rossetti was perhaps the most famous writer from the period who was involved in both the visual and the literary, in *Essays from the "Guardian,"* Pater notes that Browning had considered being a painter and a musician in addition to being a poet. In Symons's study of Pater, Symons likewise notes that Pater's own art criticism was so good that he could have made it his primary occupation.[45] This active interest in the art of the time—and its interactions with literature—had a significant influence on Wilde.[46] From the "Lecture to Art Students" to the introduction of the characters as paintings at the beginning of *An Ideal Husband* (1895) to the discussions of painters that take up sometimes-long sections of *Intentions*, Wilde's work consists of an on-going debate about the relationship between the visual and the verbal. One important part of this theorizing—especially in relation to Schlegel's work—was Wilde's use of synesthesia: a trope that provides a concrete illustration of the romantic doctrine of the fusion of the arts as it was inherited by Wilde.

Edouard Roditi traces Wilde's interests in synesthesia from the fairy tales, prose poems, and poetry to *Salomé*, which he sees as the culmina-tion of a particular tradition of synesthesia: "Ever since the Eighteenth Century, when it [synesthesia] had inspired scientific and mechanical experiments such as the Abbé Castel's color-organ or Diderot's investi-gations of blindness, the theory of synaesthesia, according to which one sense is able to perceive what appeals to another sense, had haunted the whole tradition of European Romanticism."[47] Roditi goes on to give as examples Hoffmann, Leopardi, Balzac, Rossetti, Baudelaire, Rimbaud, and, of course, Huysmans.[48] J. E. Chamberlin concurs with Roditi's assessment of Wilde's experimentation with, and interest in, painting with words and goes so far as to say that with *Salomé* and *La Sainte Courtisane*, which Chamberlin sees as directly connected to Wilde's prose poetry, he founded a "new literary genre."[49] The prose poetry, for Chamberlin, not only is an experiment with the border or barrier between poetry and prose but also acts as a place where Wilde practices various forms of literature.[50]

One need look no further than the opening of *Dorian Gray* to find a dramatic example of what Wilde had learned about synesthesia. The book begins with a catalog of visual effects described with words whose assonance and consonance call attention to their exaggerated sounds:

> The studio was filled with the rich odour of roses, and when the light summer wind stirred amidst the trees of the garden, there came through the open door the heavy scent of the lilac. . . . From the corner of the divan . . . Lord Henry Wotton could just catch the gleam of the honey-sweet and honey-coloured blossoms of a laburnum, whose tremulous branches seemed hardly able to bear the burden of a beauty so flame-like as theirs; and now and then the fantastic shadows of birds in flight flitted across the long tussore-silk curtains . . . producing a kind of momentary Japanese effect. . . . The sullen murmur of the bees . . . with monotonous insistence . . . seemed to make the stillness more oppressive. The dim roar of London was like the bourdon note of a distant organ.[51]

To a large extent, the theme of the relationship of the visual (Dorian's portrait as painted by Basil, but also painting in general) to the temporal or verbal is raised with this brilliantly overdone opening. The sensory imagery has links to the poetry of Mallarmé and the poems by Wilde that attempt to mimic the effects of the Symbolistes. Poems such as "Symphony in Yellow," "Impression de Voyage," and "Le Jardin des Tuileries" are almost wholly descriptive. The visual is in competition with other elements and contains within it the refutation of the temporal, of plot, and perhaps even psychology and the usually assumed strengths of the novel form.[52]

The prose style evoked here, with its emphasis on sensory effects, is similar to the one Wilde employed in his fairy tales such as "The Young King." However, Wilde increases the intensity of the style and places it at the service of a more complex thematic. This reconsideration of the language of prose seems to involve a reconsideration of the relationship not only between the verbal and the visual, time and space, but between poetry and prose—the ability of language to include, in as compact a form as possible, the full force of sound, image, and meaning. Certainly purple passages such as those found in the exposition of *Dorian Gray* seem to go beyond Wilde's prose poems, which themselves seem to prefigure the novel.[53] In *A Rebours*, Huysmans had already marked this form as important.[54] For Des Esseintes, the prose poet should be able to transfer "Da Vinci's methods to prose and [paint] with his metallic oxides a series of little pictures whose brilliant tints glitter like transparent enamels."[55] Baudelaire, Mallarmé, and Verlaine are, not surprisingly, among his favorite poets.[56] In "Pen, Pencil, and Poison," Wilde echoes Huysmans's conclusion: "The conception of making a prose-poem out of paint is excellent. Much of the best modern literature springs from the same aim. In a very ugly and sensible age, the arts borrow, not from life, but from each other."[57]

Wilde's attempts in *Dorian Gray* and *Salomé* to push the boundary between prose and poetry, between cognition and sonority, are indebted to the poetry of Swinburne, who, like Hopkins, believed that "words have to transgress their limits and move beyond the boundaries constituted for them." One way Swinburne attempted to do this, as Isobel Armstrong explains, was by his

> habit of doubling a word with an alliterative synonym, and doubling that synonymous double with a synonymous alliterative phrase, [as] a way of

dissolving the boundaries of language by coalescing distinctions of sound and meaning. The synonym chain produces an endless chain of substitution in which doubled words and phrases blur and exchange semantic and aural attributes with libidinal energy, impelled by an insistent and self-perpetuating metrical form.[58]

Swinburne's experimentation with this formal problem was in the service of a larger goal. As the self-proclaimed "English Baudelaire,"[59] his "affirmation through negation" in *Poems and Ballads* constitutes "the realignment, the recalibration so to speak, of vice and virtue, freedom and oppression, male and female, homosexual, heterosexual, and the questioning of these oppositions" to create "a unique project in the poetry of the 1860s and 1870s."[60]

For Schlegel, the novel was a new type of autobiographical form that required more from the reader, or the audience, than other forms of art precisely because it broke up "the fictional illusion but also [opened] up space for the response of the audience and its inclusion into the making of the work."[61] The sections of dialogue, sudden shifts in generic form, and use of fragments that can be seen in *Lucinde* allow for not only the prefiguring of a Brechtian mode of work for the audience to engage in—a sort of writing as performance art piece—but also the attempt "to negate the abyss between subject and object."[62] The ironic mode for Wilde is perhaps even more complicated in that by the time one gets to *Earnest* all the characters utter epigrams in a display of dandical discourse that leaves everything destabilized and in a constant process of becoming rather than being: a perfect parabasis. As early as "The Portrait of Mr. W. H." there is an inkling of the same structure in nascent form. As Gagnier notes, the essay "presents a dialogical production of a theory through three separate advocates, and the narrator's ambivalence at the end emphasizes its unfinalizability."[63] All the characters talk as their author does, in other words, though each represents only one fragment of his combined discourse. The middle part of Wilde's career, therefore, represents a trajectory toward a pure ironic mode— one in which the creation of a new form, in *Earnest*, is the telos.

If *Dorian Gray* prefigures Wilde's social comedies, it is in the concept of the persona—the trope of the mask—that Wilde's greatest debt to Schlegel might be found. Lilian P. Furst notes that "with the romantic ironist the mask merges with the persona in a displacement likely to generate disorientation."[64] Certainly this was true for Wilde, even though his public persona at the time of the novel's writing was still that of an aesthete rather than a homosexual. Wilde's novel can be read as a criticism of the life that follows the dictates of Paterian aestheticism. Yet the preface, one of the supreme documents of aesthetic literature, and the "gay" subplot belie the moralistic main plot of the novel. It can be argued, in fact, that *Dorian Gray* is an example of Wilde's attempt to try on different masks: the Victorian family man, the critic and theorizer of aesthetics, the soon-to-be-revealed homosexual of the demimonde. "The Truth of Masks" and "The Portrait of Mr. W. H." both deal with revelation, and in the latter, what is revealed is something like homosexuality. What the novel suggests is the same: the closet is the open signifier waiting to be found by the discerning reader. Instability via sexuality and identity, then, becomes an aspect of Wilde's inheritance of romantic irony. If the ultimate goal of German romanticism and of Wilde's philosophy was to make objective forms expressive—the ultimate way to express self—then the use of the mask was an ideal way to do this. In "The Critic as Artist," Wilde states, "Yes, the objective form is the most subjective in matter. Man is least himself when he talks in his own person. Give him a mask, and he will tell you the truth."[65] In "The Truth of Masks," he concludes that "the truths of metaphysics are the truths of masks."[66] The epistemological significance of the closet becomes the masked truth about which Wilde writes in *Dorian Gray* and elsewhere.[67] Both Tennyson and Browning went on to write with masks—in the form of monologues—after supposedly outgrowing their "aestheticist" periods.[68] The metamorphosis of aestheticism's poses into a playing with masks suggests a movement from aestheticism to protoqueer decadence.

The use of a mask—whether in the form of a dramatic monologue or a persona in a dialogue—had to do not only with the monologuistic tendency of the preferred creative and philosophical forms of the nineteenth century but also with a steady disassociation, as Carol T. Christ observes, of the poet from the speaker that may have resulted, ultimately, in the objectivity of Eliot and Pound. This very telos, however, also shows the extent to which the modernist poets are not only heirs to the romantic period but are also inextricably linked to the Victorian poems whose influences they so wish to guard themselves against. Each period's artists—romantic, Victorian, and modernist—constructed a version of the preceding period for their own use. Wilde's construction of romanticism had everything to do with his own self-invention as a type from that period: a new Byron or Disraeli for his time. As Christ notes:

> Wilde's concept of the mask shows a number of shifts in emphasis from Browning's and Tennyson's development of the dramatic monologue. What was an implicit emphasis . . . upon objectivity and freedom from the limitations of a single poetic voice becomes in Wilde an explicit program for life as well as for art. Wilde does not emphasize the separation between the man and his work that for Tennyson and Browning constituted the chief advantage of the dramatic monologue. Rather, he insists on the connection between the man and his masks. While Tennyson and Browning used the dramatic monologue both to express and evade the limitation of personality, Wilde uses the concept of the mask to transcend it. He emphasizes not the poet's distance from his voices, but the experience those voices allow him to encompass.[69]

Wilde not only extends the use of the mask beyond that of his immediate contemporaries but also reestablishes it as the self-conscious center of his aesthetics. Just as the mask existed for Schlegel as the most important vehicle for irony, so for Wilde the mask was essential for creativity, for the ability to formulate the ultimate form of "truth."

Toward the end of chapter 13 of *Dorian Gray*, our protagonist disposes of Basil Hallward's coat and travel bag in "a secret press . . . in which he kept his own curious disguises."[70] Dorian has just murdered Basil—the book's one true artist and the creator of Dorian's portrait—

and the disguises that Dorian mentions are real ones. Forced by his own corruption of Basil's creation to live as a reflection not of his own soul but of Basil's desire for him, Dorian resorts to the basest means possible to attempt to pass in society. Part of the irony is that Dorian's own face is now a mask—one that hides a soul in trouble. The reference to a mask or a disguise is also one of many references to Dorian's vague "sins"— blackmail, drug use, even vampirism are a few either hinted at or named. All may well be a stand-in for, or displacement of, homosexuality.

The thematics of the mask allow Wilde not only to create three main characters all of whom seem to reflect aspects of Wilde's own public persona, but also to make everyone in the novel wear a mask of some type. Sybil's family is composed of stock characters from melodrama. Just as Sybil is nothing without her stage personae, her mother would not exist if she had not already starred in numerous bad productions. Harry is the essence of the self-invented dandy whose philosophy of "hedonism" so infects Dorian's ego. Dorian is himself both bifurcated and hollowed out—neither wholly human nor ever completely more than the signifier of a split in the concept of identity as it existed at the time of the novel's conception. Wilde's masks are metamasks, performances that comment on performance and on the impossibility of ever resolving the split between the public and the private articulations of self.

Wilde's use of the mask makes the reader self-conscious of the artificiality of his undertaking—of the mixing of modes of discourse throughout. Not only does the novel hold at its center an unresolvable difference between painting and prose—illusion and realism—but throughout the novel, Wilde is commenting on Huysmans, most especially in chapter 11, which consists almost completely of lists and seems to be an attempt on Wilde's part to place within his novel an homage to the static nature of Huysmans's *Au Rebours*. Wilde likewise interpolates into his text entire sections that consist of banter and repartee between characters at parties or at dinner. Wilde makes clear early on that Harry's ability to hold his guests' attention merely by his conversational skills marks the verbal as particularly telling, as these moments flatten out the realism of the text—putting it momentarily on hold by stopping the plot and adding little to the actual unfolding of the narrative itself. The seduction that Harry begins in Basil's garden—one that is composed of "mere words" and is taken over, eventually, by the book that Harry gives to Dorian—is completed in the company of others:

> A laugh ran round the table.
>
> He [Lord Henry] played with the idea, and grew wilful; tossed it into the air and transformed it; let it escape and recaptured it; made it iridescent with fancy, and winged with paradox. . . .
>
> Dorian never took his gaze off him, but sat like one under a spell. . . .
>
> At last . . . Reality entered the room in the shape of a servant.[71]

Realism is that which brings an end to merriment. To live as Dorian lives—at least for a time—is to exist outside the laws of nature, beyond the control of realism. Wilde allows the reader the experience that Wilde was attempting in real life. The portrait that Wilde paints of Harry is one that Wilde has famously said reflects how the world sees him. Certainly, as a description of Wilde as a teller of tales, Harry's moments seem the most autobiographical. The points in the text where his conversation is either described or recounted are, paradoxically, the most realistic, as though what we are reading could have been a transcript from real life—from the life that we know Wilde led.

When Dorian first meets Harry's wife, Lady Henry, she knows him from the photographs that Harry keeps. Dorian's image is not only already reproduced in Basil's portrait—which almost no one has seen—but also apparently by this new process of exposure. Their conversation turns to music, and Lady Henry notes that she admires "good music": "I adore it, but I am afraid of it. It makes me too romantic. I have simply worshipped pianists."[72] Lady Henry's admission is not only telling—the idea that one could be "too romantic," in a text like this, seems unlikely—but suggests that Lady Henry is capable of worshipping the performer, not the text. Wilde's own trajectory after this novel would be toward the breakdown of the distinction between the two. Romanticism, like realism, is finally just another mode of existence for Wilde—another style. Romanticism is what you have to do when the age becomes too realistic—or when life itself finally becomes too full of choices. Romanticism begins where the mirror ends.

Romanticism was criticized by Gautier in France in favor of Parnassianism and by Disraeli and Bulwer-Lytton as something to be gotten over in favor of Victorianism. If romanticism was seen at best as a passing phase to be outgrown, moving beyond it to something else helped to protect these early practicers of dandyism and decadence from public scandal, from a shifting from effeminacy to the register of the recently named concept of homosexuality. The novels of Disraeli, for example, are a recording of his own performance—different sections of a bildungsroman that he actually acted out as he moved from romanticism to politics and simultaneously discarded the more epicene pretenses of the dandy and began to criticize their effects in his novels.[73] German romanticism had provided support for the early French and English dandies' experiments with prose and genre. By the time of Wilde, the inheritance of the Jena group provided him with a significantly different concept of romanticism to use when developing his own work and thought. That the epistemological instability that existed around his performance of gender and sexuality was mirrored in his work is by now a given. My contention is that much of this mapping from one onto the other follows a pattern begun by Schlegel—that it is, indeed, a perfection or at least a continuation of it. The trials were, in fact, an attempt to stabilize the subtle relationship that Wilde established between his work and his life by turning Wilde himself into the "type" of himself, or rather, the realignment of his signification into what would become "homosexual" as the new age of romance that Wilde had declared was quickly brought to an extremely realistic end.

though it is the least often performed of his plays today, and that his projects, had they continued, would have been informed by a new social consciousness that—though always obliquely present in his work—would come to the fore in *Reading Gaol*. That *Earnest* represented a new art form was not at all clear to him. Indeed, one only need look at the original four-act version to see that *Earnest* would have been more like his previous Ibsen-like plays had he not been forced to change the structure—and, most especially, the pacing—by George Alexander.[1] Similarly, Wilde's notion of what his work was to become was changed forever by the experience of prison. Two years of hard labor, as Wayne Koestenbaum notes, gave "birth" to "gay reading."

In his biography of Wilde, Richard Ellmann records the following letter that Wilde sent to Ernest Dowson, who had persuaded him to sleep with a woman again, which Wilde did—a prostitute in Dieppe: "The first these ten years, and it shall be the last. It was like chewing cold mutton . . . . But tell it in England, where it will entirely restore my reputation."[2] Wilde's life after prison became one in which his attachment to Douglas had never really ceased; rather, for all the financial hardships he suffered, Wilde seemed to realize that he was not only forced to reinvent himself but should not attempt to restore whatever had been there before. His life instead took on a different feel and look: he lived with Douglas without any pretense to being married or a "family man"; as the quoted letter indicates, he seemed to consolidate his sexuality to a same-sex rather than a cross-sex model;[3] his forays into the international queer subculture (his friendships with von Gloeden and Gide, for example) became much more public as he met various "notorious" figures on the Continent much as he had before, but with gay subject matter as a point of common interest; he assumed, for the first time in his life, a quasi-anonymous identity: first as the prison designation "C. 3. 3.," then as "Sebastian Melmouth," a reference to Saint Sebastian (a gay icon) and to *Melmouth the Wanderer* (1820), a novel written by Charles Maturin, his maternal great-uncle.[4] In other words, for the first time, Wilde did not merely reinvent himself as another version of himself—as what he performed regularly as "Oscar Wilde"—but rather became another person altogether, a type that, one might argue, was a simulacrum that was to become known as "the homosexual."

In part, this theory of change is the argument advanced by Koestenbaum when he says that

> in the letter he [Wilde] wrote from prison to his lover, Lord Alfred Douglas (Bosie), "In Carcere et Vinculis" (posthumously titled *De Profundis*), and in the poem he wrote after release, "The Ballad of Reading Gaol," Wilde gestured toward . . . a gay male reader and suggested that "gay identity" is constructed through reading, although once it has been located on the page, it glows like an essence that already existed *before* a reader's glance brought it to life.[5]

Although Koestenbaum is well aware of the potential essentializing that is being constructed in his reading of the cultural work done by Wilde's final pieces of writing, the most important point to keep in mind is his claim that Wilde consciously attempted to invent a reader—one implied by his text. More specifically, Koestenbaum is interested in how Wilde turned his prison experience into a new code of signification— the gay male—that his name and his person were ultimately to have applied to them.

Koestenbaum argues effectively that Wilde's first piece of writing under this new regime of signification, his letter from prison, places the reader in the position of the absent lover, Bosie. Wilde's attack on him can be seen as a reflection of what Wilde imagined as the "type" of the young gay lover, "indolent" and vain, but it was also an attempt by Wilde at an actual portrait of a real Dorian—to make public and visible, in other words, the type whose silence the letter inevitably meets and attempts to transcend.[6] In this sense, the private nature of a letter is made purposefully public as Wilde counters his own incarceration with a letter written by Douglas with a letter of his own in which he attempts not only to explain himself but, as Koestenbaum argues, to define the type that he has become—to take control of it—by projecting it through the letter and onto Douglas and, in doing so, creating a portrait both of him and of the gay man that the letter presumes will be its "canniest reader."[7] As "one of the first texts ever written with the knowledge that it would be seen as the work of an 'exposed' gay man," Wilde's letter is not so much a confession as an attempt via a writerly performance to transform a reading (or reader) into something gay.

Koestenbaum extends his argument to the question of Wilde's concern for the reproduction of his letter for the outside—that is, non-prison—world. Playing on the idea of reproduction as the reproducing of the labor that Wilde's prison forced him to endure, Koestenbaum claims that Wilde found reproduction not in engendering an essential gay self but rather by "cloning" himself via the literal reproduction in book form of *Reading Gaol* in 1898—the typing, typesetting, designing, and printing of it, all of which Koestenbaum shows that Wilde had a great interest in. Likewise, the publication of *Reading Gaol* became a way not only to replicate Wilde as a type—as typing—but even to re-create him, to conjure his spirit as both the originary model for homosexuality and as a celebrity, however notorious or controversial he may have become in the wake of twentieth-century homophobic attitudes.

Indeed, Wilde's success as a type has everything to do with his awareness of himself as a commodity after the trial—and of his awareness of the importance of self-dramatization and self-promotion before it. Koestenbaum sees Wilde as a postmodern figure of the Warhol variety: a proto-1970s clone who knew how to keep his fifteen minutes of fame going by first metamorphosing into whatever would sell and then, after his release, selling the self that had been created by the context that society imposed on him. Wilde's infamy became the selling point for his books, in other words, at least as much as the works "themselves." As Neil Bartlett notes, the detective story that so often is the explicit or implicit part of Wilde's writing—the hunt for a type, the encoding of a milieu— becomes not only explicit after the trial but also something that is capable of being copied and distributed as a new type for a new century.[8]

The version of history created by Wilde in *De Profundis* is, of course, a recounting of his time with Douglas during the years before his trials. In *Reading Gaol*, Koestenbaum argues, Wilde creates not so much a history as a new lexical map of the road ahead, a new way to *read* the history of which he is now, inextricably, a part. In the juxtaposition of criminal argot with that of gay men, Wilde creates a reader who bridges the distance between Wilde, the speaker of the poem, and the man who is hanged in the poem—the dedicatee, C[harles]. T[homas]. W[ooldridge]. The Christlike figure that Wilde becomes at the end of *De Profundis* is here applied to Wooldridge, who not only "kills the thing he loves" but becomes the objective correlative for the suffering of all the men in the prison—the "we" of which the reader is made a part. That these sufferers are also the men imprisoned by society's mores about homosexuality is clearly Koestenbaum's primary point, and the place at which Wilde's creation of a type—criminal, homosexual— is meant to be an attempt at transcending his historical moment to project "his revarnished reputation" into the future. Wilde both predicts his own resurrection in the public's memory and stages his own Calvary by fashioning a new mythology for himself as an emerging type that is "forming" around his name just as Wooldridge's identity allowed for the creation of this ballad—the excuse for the recognition of an evil done to one and to many.

The Uses of Orientalism: *Teleny*

> The desire of the eye to see itself seeing with no blind spots, with nothing behind it, is the formula for paranoia, for Romantic irony, and for the Oriental tale, a self-reflexive narrative with notes.
>
> —Jerome Christensen, *Lord Byron's Strength*

As suggested by Koestenbaum, it is tempting to view the community of prisoners as a metaphor for the new type that Wilde had not only become but also, perhaps, inaugurated. Ed Cohen and Alan Sinfield are just two among the many critics who have traced the ways in which Wilde's name became a literal metaphor for the new scientific definition of the homosexual. That is, Wilde's name acted as a powerful designation for most of the discussion of male-male attraction—and, in a sense, created it simply by providing a name. In preparing *Reading Gaol* to be published, "Wilde observed this happening when he accepted . . . that it might be a good idea to publish . . . anonymously. 'As regards America, I think it would be better now to publish there *without* my name. I see it is my *name* that terrifies.'"[9] The use of no name—or actually his prison nom de plume—allowed Wilde to call more attention to the book because of the secret that the misnomer inevitably implied. That this secret was a transparent one that yet allowed the reader "an alibi" was clear to Wilde: "The public like an open secret."

For Sinfield, Wilde's trials did not create a type so much as solidify one. The bisexual dandy of aestheticism and decadence became, with Wilde, an exclusively male-centered sexual being whose effeminacy—whether pose or not—functioned to signify and advertise this new type.[10] Though Sinfield attempts to tease out the complexity of this transition and to indicate the inability ever to stabilize the "moment" of its emergence, he does seem to prefer thinking of the myriad definitions of the time—from "urning" to "invert," for example—as marking the period as queer: a time in which the attempt to stop the flow of definitions succeeded only in establishing their primary characteristics as a type in Wilde, though this type was clearly unstable and capable of change, as one sees by the varying nature of the self-identification by gay men throughout the subsequent twentieth century and up to a return, in the present time, to a new notion of "queer."

Sinfield is careful, in fact, to caution against designating the "moment" crystallized by and around Wilde as one in which it is possible to map a one-to-one correspondence onto our own. Though Wilde as a figure may have been uniting communities of people engaged in producing a discourse about same-sex desire, the trope of Wilde was not necessarily acting as the specific prototype of our own age. That is, it is simply wrong to see Wilde or his friends as an origin that the actions of gay men in this age have somehow created. Instead, Wilde's own queer moment is a historical one that must be seen within the social and material contexts of Wilde's life and experiences. For instance, it seems unlikely that Wilde or anyone at that time would have imagined wanting to politicize the mainly medical identity that was to form around the concept of "homosexual" shortly after Wilde's trial and exile. This resistance on Sinfield's part to claiming Wilde as an originary center of twentieth-century gay identity is an argument that he perhaps takes too far at times, but which nevertheless makes it easier to ask more accurate questions about how Wilde's emergence as a type was formative for the queer discourse of subsequent times.[11]

It might seem odd to argue that as someone who spent most of his life trying desperately not to be anonymous, Wilde would seek that status even after his infamous trial. However, Wilde may very well have believed that one can derive almost as much from not being known as from being known.[12] He was obviously able to accomplish as much by not naming homosexual desire in *Dorian Gray*—at least directly—as he would have by naming it. Therefore the claim that Wilde established and named a new type after his acceptance of its formation in prison needs substantiation. One possible way to do this is to look, as Koestenbaum does, at the relationship of the literary to Wilde's material interest in the editions of the two postprison writings. However, what might be more enabling in an attempt to find in Wilde a pattern for the future is to look not at his quasi-anonymous work like *Gaol* but at what could be his actual anonymous work: his editing and/or writing of *Teleny* and the attributed translations.

In one of the diaristic entries in his book on Wilde, Bartlett tries to convince himself that "The Portrait of Mr. W. H." is not really about "the origin of Shakespeare's sonnets at all" but "about our origins as homosexual men. At the very moment at which, historically, we begin to exist, he created a biography of a homosexual man in which the fake and the true are quite indistinguishable. He proposed that our present is continually being written by our history; that the individual voice can hardly be separated from the historic text which it repeats and adapts."[13] If Wilde did contribute to *Teleny*—as a coauthor and/or editor—then this formulation may well suggest the spirit in which he engaged in that project. Though the attribution of Wilde's hand to the prose style has been made by Winston Leyland, among others, there are few if any definite clues in the novel that Wilde was part of the actual writing. Though it is exciting to think that he may have written *Teleny* as a sort of "reverse" of *Dorian Gray* in which all that is (to some extent) covered in that novel is here exposed, a more probable argument can be made that Wilde was the editor or "instigator," as Leyland puts it, of a sub-cultural documentary project—one that required that he be anonymous, collaborative, and but one actor in a community that formed, in essence, a secret society.[14]

The title page of the first edition of *Teleny* gives the full title as *Teleny, or The Reverse of the Medal: A Physiological Romance*, with the place of publication as "Cosmopoli." The anonymity of the fictitious place suggests a city center—or, rather, multiple urban places, perhaps pointing toward the collective experiences of centuries of "gay" men in urban settings—a sort of homosexual continuum such as Bartlett envisions for London. The place of origin also suggests an international conspiracy of place, hence the possibility that the novel, in its ultimate form, was composed in several places, or at least by several different men. The title likewise offers clues about the book's meaning. Though "Teleny" refers to the protagonist's name, "the reverse of the medal" alludes to the title of the first story of *Les Cent Nouvelles nouvelles* (the hundred new stories), which is usually referred to as the French version of the *Decameron*.[15] Supposedly written by thirty-five noblemen, some of the tales are re-tellings of Boccaccio, Poggio, and various French *fabliaux*, while some are stories published for the first time. Like the anonymous and semi-anonymous writings of the *Decameron*, many of the tales come from an oral tradition. The primary example for this type of collection, however, is not a Western one but rather the non-Western, "Oriental" example of *The Tales of the Thousand Nights and a One*, which existed by the time of *Teleny*'s writing in the famous 1885 edition by Sir Richard Burton. Containing the famous "Terminal Essay," which explained the frequent prevalence of "pederasty" in the many sexual actions enumerated in the tales, the Orient, as conceived of by Wilde's peers, would have provided an obvious paradigm for just such a transgressive representation of ex-plicit sexuality and sex as one has in *Les Cent Nouvelles nouvelles*.

At the beginning of chapter 4 of *Dorian Gray*, *Les Cent Nouvelles* is one of the objects mentioned as the centerpiece of Lord Henry's "little library" in Mayfair: "On a tiny satinwood table stood a statuette by Clodion, and beside it lay a copy of *Les Cent Nouvelles*, bound for Margaret of Valois by Clovis Eve, and powdered with the gilt daisies that Queen had selected for her device."[16] Indeed, like the book that Lord Henry read at age sixteen, or the mysterious "novel without a plot" at the end of chapter 10,[17] or the "little vellum-covered book" by Gautier in chapter 9,[18] *Les Cent Nouvelles* is one of the many books that complete the education begun by Lord Henry—one in which Dorian discovers "the sins of the world . . . passing in a dumb show before him. Things that he had dimly dreamed of were suddenly made real to him. Things of which he had never dreamed were gradually revealed."[19] The paragraph that follows this description makes clear that Wilde had in mind Huysmans's novel, as can be gleaned by the accuracy with which he describes it—including its ability to create for Dorian a narrative of innocence that is transformed into secret knowledge, which suggests the pornographic model provided by *Les Cent Nouvelles* and *Teleny*.

Writing the introduction to the first English translation of *The Hundred Stories* in 1899, Robert B. Douglas proposed the theory that the collection of tales was narrated at the exile court of the dauphin, Louis XI, who stayed with Phillipe Le Bon from 1456 to 1461, during the time that he was estranged from his father, Charles VII. Later, perhaps in 1467, "the tales were written down . . . by a literary man, and they owe 'the crispness, fluency, and elegance'" to him.[20] Indeed, this "literary man," someone educated beyond the tellers of the tales, could have been Louis himself, Duke Philippe, or—as was argued at the time—the duke's subject Antoine de La Salle, whose prose style is apparently discernible at places in the book. Comte de Charolais (later, Charles le Temeraire, the final duke of Burgundy) was also suggested as the author by some Victorian scholars. What is clear is that someone edited and selected the stories, though the authorship, when Douglas was writing, was hotly contested.

At the time of *Teleny*, the 1858 edition of *The Hundred Stories*, published by Jannet in Paris, had been issued, though only someone who could read French would have been familiar with the collection and its contested authorship. Though contemporary scholars attribute the editorship to Philippe de Vigneulles and his compiling of them as occurring between 1505 and 1515, the model for authorship that the 1858 edition would have provided was exactly the same as the one that *Teleny* was to copy with its appearance in 1893.[21] In fact, the use of the subtitle to refer to *Les Cent Nouvelles* may have been an attempt to suggest not only the rowdy nature of *Teleny* but also that the story of the authorship of *Teleny* is of the same nature as that of *Les Cent Nouvelles*; that is, the controversy surrounding the origins of *Les Cent Nouvelles* may have been planted self-consciously as a clue to the authorship of *Teleny* by that book's editor.[22]

If Wilde is the editor, connecting *Les Cent Nouvelles* to Lord Henry in *Dorian Gray* makes clear that a knowledge of *The Hundred Stories* was considered not merely esoteric and somewhat scandalous but also queer and sophisticated. "Inside" knowledge, in other words, is the hallmark of the book's function in the telling of Dorian's story. Similarly, *Teleny* may well serve an analogous role in Wilde's career. Unlike *Dorian Gray* or other of Wilde's more explicitly homoerotic works, *Teleny* makes sex between men abundantly visible and unmistakable. Wilde's contribution to the creation of *Teleny* might function as a hidden clue or key to his other work. The original bookseller's prospectus describes *Teleny* as a book that though "dealing with scenes which surpass in freedom the wildest licence, the culture of its author's style adds an additional piquancy and spice to the narration."[23] Although this description refers to a single author, it also makes the point that the author is one of "culture" and, we would assume, education and influence. The intellectual or high-culture nature of the book is further alluded to by a reference to John Addington Symonds's theories about sexuality— which at the same time would have made it clear that the actual author could not be Symonds, who had just died, yet must be someone who is acquainted with his work. Indeed, though not named, Wilde would have been one of the few people in England that this rather open secret could possibly name.

Two complete accounts of the publishing history of *Teleny* are extant. The first was provided by H. Montgomery Hyde in his 1966 introduction to an English edition, and the second by Leyland in the 1984 Gay Sunshine Press edition. In his updating of Hyde, Leyland attempts to reconcile the discrepancies between the 1934 French edition and the original edition from 1893 while also raising once again the problems of authorial attribution. His narrative of the book's creation therefore has two parts: Hyde's theory about how the book was written between 1890 and 1893; and the story of the book's subsequent publication in two different versions—one in English and one in French. Leyland quotes Hyde's summary of Charles Hirsch's introduction to the French edition, which provides an account of the book's writing and much of its connection to Wilde. Hirsch claims that Wilde frequented his bookshop, Librairie Parisienne, after it opened in London in 1889. A frequent purchaser of Zola and Maupassant, Wilde later began to buy "certain licentious works of a special *genre* which he euphemistically described as 'socratic' and which the bookseller was able to obtain." Apparently Wilde's tastes did not run to the hard-core, as he rejected some books "whose crudity evidently displeased," though he did purchase one book in English: *The Sins of the Cities of the Plain* (1881), "which purported to be an autobiographical account of a male homosexual's experience in contemporary London."[24] Indeed, Hirsch suggests that this book became one of the models for *Teleny*, as shortly thereafter—"towards the end of 1890"—Wilde brought in "a small package" with the instructions that it would be picked up by another person, who would show his card. Again, according to Hirsch, this happened three times until, finally, he opened the package the last time it was returned because the wrapping was by then gone and the manuscript was "simply tied around with a piece of ribbon."[25] What Hirsch found was a title page "with a single word 'Teleny,'" but also a manuscript that was filled with an "extraordinary mixture of different handwriting, erasures, interlineations, corrections and additions by various hands." In fact, the only conclusion to draw, thought Hirsch, was that Wilde's friends wrote it and that Wilde himself "supervised and corrected the manuscript, adding touches of his own here and there."[26] A textual analysis of the book's narrative style, while not substantiating this theory, also does not rule it out.

In fact, when the novel was published three years later by Leonard Smithers, Hirsch noticed few changes in the text, though, on the title page, there was the addition of the subtitle and of "Cosmopoli" as the place of publication. The subtitle would seem to point to Wilde as the author—an emblem placed on the text to indicate his involvement with it. The place of publication, similarly, is also a reference to Wilde's friend and collaborator Aubrey Beardsley, who often stayed at the Cosmopolitani in Menton, on the Riviera, where Smithers often wrote to him. The publication, in other words, only confirms the book's creation by and for a coterie—the educated gay clientele for whom von Gloeden and others created same-sex male pornography. The first printing of *Teleny* ran to only two hundred copies.[27]

The original manuscript for *Teleny* does not exist. One must therefore trust these accounts, as they, along with the printed texts, constitute all the evidence. How much the publishers may have altered the text is known, apparently, only to Hirsch, Smithers, and the French publisher. Hirsch does say that Smithers admitted to him that he transposed some of the action from London to Paris in order to make the book call less attention to itself upon publication, though he planned to publish the original manuscript, which he possessed, with the next edition.[28] Unfortunately Smithers never lived to do this, though someone did see that Hirsch came into possession of the manuscript.[29] The manuscript then disappeared, though the French edition of 1934 (possibly published by Marcel Scheur, probably translated by Hirsch) with Hirsch's introduction is apparently based on the original manuscript. *Teleny*, therefore, was published in its original form not in English but in French. As with Wilde's *Salomé*, it is in French that one must find the representation of such extreme "perversity" and decadence, and Paris the place to which one flees for sexual liberation.

If Wilde is the author or the editor/author of the book, then why was he so careful not to leave more numerous—though perhaps equally subtle—clues as to his identity? Hirsch's argument is that Wilde would have feared any hint of exposure from this project, as it was written when he was married, had two children, and was trying hard to make a career. Indeed, around 1890, Wilde was still a couple of years away from his first real financial success, which came with *Lady Windermere's Fan*. It is, however, the time in which, via *Dorian Gray*, he began to experiment with the creation of homoerotic situations in his creative work. Likewise, it is around this time that Hirsch visited Wilde at his home in Chelsea and noted that "unusual details of furniture, curtains, and general decoration corresponded fairly closely to similar descriptions he had read in the manuscript of *Teleny*."[30] Indeed, Wilde's home was a famous showplace for the more avant-garde ideas then in vogue about home furnishings—a topic that he spoke about at length during his North American lecture tour just before marrying and settling down in London. Hirsch's observations therefore make the point that there is support for Wilde's involvement in the text of the novel, but that the connections are not easy ones to make.[31]

Whether or not Wilde is the "secondary author" or is simply associated with the project, the point is that both his life and his reputation were being connected to the book at the time and, perhaps more significantly, after his death and into the twentieth century. The desire to attribute the book to Wilde is a palpable part of the history of the introduction of the category of "homosexual" at the end of the nineteenth century. If Wilde could be linked directly to the book, it would seem to provide the certainty that the late twentieth century would like to have that Wilde is indeed the origin of contemporary gay identity. It may be enough, however, to realize that Wilde exists for this book as a sort of symbolic presence—someone whose identity, name, or performative persona acts as the inspiration for the common interpretation of the book and whose very life becomes emblematic of a certain kind of pathos that the book evokes in a contemporary reader, especially one whose interpretation of a nascent gay identity might be especially keen. It may be more important, therefore, to see the book as a collective or collaborative effort, not just as the product of a coterie but as something created by men not only so they could negotiate various identities and fictions as fantasy but also as a way to enjoy each other, to be held in a common enjoyment of bodies in pleasure.[32]

"Tell me your story from its very beginning, Des Grieux, said he, interrupting me; and how you got to be acquainted with him."[33] The novel begins, like *The Hundred Stories*, with a story being told to a listener; the substance of the story—"how you got to be acquainted with him"—is the same one asked by Wilde in *De Profundis*: When did this man enter my life and how? The first chapter recounts the meeting of the handsome young pianist, Teleny, and the flaneur Des Grieux by way of an introduction by a mutual friend, Bryancourt, who is described as one of several of "a few dandies . . . grouped round a young man in evening dress."[34] The man turns out to be Teleny, and the conversation soon turns to the question of what would define "a sympathetic listener" for his music. The reader has earlier been privy to a dreamy section in which Des Grieux narrates how he was "spell-bound" upon hearing Teleny play and unable to "tell whether it [the cause of the effect] was with the composition, the execution, or the player himself."[35] The conversation between Teleny and Bryancourt soon turns into a test for Teleny as Bryancourt describes a vision of "some beautiful girl": "Two lily-white breasts with nipples like two pink rosebuds, and lower down, two moist lips like those pink shells which, opening with awakening lust, reveal a pulpy, luxurious world, only of a deep coralline hue."[36] After repeatedly asking Teleny if this would be his listener, Teleny finally answers, "perhaps," while Des Grieux "smile[s], thinking how different my vision has been from these." Teleny responds: "My vision was very different." To which Bryancourt says: "Then it [the vision of the listener] must have been *le revers de la médaille*—the back side . . . that is, two snow-clad lovely hillocks and deep in the valley below, a well, a tiny hole with a dark margin, or rather a brown halo around it." When asked again, "let us have your vision now," Teleny answers "evasively" that "my visions are so vague and indistinct, they fade away so quickly, that I can hardly remember them."[37]

The image of the breasts and vagina of a young woman is immediately transposed—reversed—into the buttocks and anus of a woman, or perhaps of a man. The reference to this reversal occurs in a narrative situation in which one man attempts to intercede for his friend to determine the sexuality of his friend's new interest by changing the "vision" of a young woman into that of a young man. The reversal includes not only a switching of sexes but also a reversal from front to back. Bryancourt refers specifically to the plot of the story in *Les Cent Nouvelles* entitled "The Reverse of the Medal," in which a man who is sleeping with his neighbor's wife fools the husband, who returns suddenly from a business trip to knock on the neighbor's door. When the husband is let in and sees the food and wine that is set out, he becomes suspicious and asks to see who is lying in the bed. The neighbor argues that for modesty's sake, he cannot show the man the face of his new bride. The husband insists, and the neighbor offers a proposal: he will show him her backside, which is "comely," if the man will be satisfied with that. The husband cannot disagree, as he is not "the master there," and comes close to the bed with a candle, only to see "the backside of his wife, and her haunches and thighs."[38] Though still suspicious, he goes home, where he finds his wife sweeping; surprised that he has returned, she berates him for his foolishness. Based on a fabliau that predates the book, this tale sets the tone for many of the stories, whose plots are linked by the image of a female backside.[39] Indeed, sexuality itself seems to be defined by this one erogenous zone—so often is it used as the single recurring synecdoche not only for a woman's sexuality but for sex itself.

"The Damsel Knight," for instance, recounts how a maiden dresses up as a man to sleep with her lover for three nights to see if she can trust him (he fails the test), and "The Scotsman Turned Washer-Woman" tells the story of a man who wears a dress for fourteen years to ingratiate himself with young women in order to sleep with them. Although both of these stories use gender disguise for heterosexual purposes, cross-dressing and homosociality are shown to be necessary for heterosexual seduction. In the former, Katherine, the woman who is in disguise, becomes Coned, who walks arm in arm with her lover, Gerard, with whom she sleeps in the same bed. Likewise, the Scotsman enjoys apparently instantaneous friendships with women, who insist that he always sleep in the same bed with them. It is only at night that he throws off his disguise and seduces them. Much more typical, however, is a story like "The Scarlet Backside," in which a woman tells her secret lover that though she saves her backside for her husband, the rest of her is for him. Or in "The Chaste Mouth," a wife gives all of her body to her lover but her mouth, as it was with her mouth that she made her vows—and thus only her mouth has pledged itself to her husband. Indeed, though "The Scarlet Backside" involves misogyny—and other stories depict castration, threat of rape by a husband, and, in "Tit for Tat," cross-generational incest—the stories have in common the reversal of body parts, indeed, the symmetrical interchangeableness of them. Whether switching partners or genders, the stories privilege reversal as the book's dominant figural trope. The wife's backside is pictured, in some illustrations of the title story, as by the head of her lover—that is, she is inverse to him, so that her backside is where her face would be "normally." Similarly, when she runs into her house before her husband arrives there, she enters through the "postern"—the rear gate or door, not through the front like her husband.[40]

Teleny takes the reversals of *The Hundred Stories* and inverts them yet further, as the depiction of sex and body parts in the novel is often, though not always, sodomical. Indeed, much like the backsides depicted in *The Hundred Stories*, the homosexual acts in *Teleny* are governed by the act of male-to-male anal sex. The bawdy humor of *Les Cent Nouvelles* is replaced with a sophisticated pornographic setting. The various examples of sexual activities—Teleny sleeping with the maid, with Des Grieux's mother, or even the famous all-male orgy scene in which there are various tableaux of men having sex in groups—are rendered in a highly visual style that focuses on the body parts in much the same way that nineteenth- and twentieth-century "pornographic" literature does. Though the novel has its own ironic distance—supplied in large part by the tone set by having the witty Des Grieux as the narrator—the rhythm of the novel's plot is fragmented into a series of scenes in which the purpose is ultimately to create a new situation in which more people can engage in sex. *Teleny*, in other words, becomes a series of stories about sex—perhaps about different men's fantasies about, or adventures of, sex—told with an overarching interest in the homoerotic attraction between its two principal protagonists.

The frame for the story, or at least the metacommentary that weaves in and out of it, is the banter between Des Grieux and the anonymous person to whom he is telling the story. The mysterious other, who seems to know a lot about the milieu and the characters Des Grieux discusses, nevertheless does not do much more than ask questions—specifically, questions that are designed to encourage Des Grieux to tell more of his story. This elaborate conceit encapsulates the novel within a dialogic structure very similar to Wilde's: one in which the "dialogue" is really simply an elaborate monologue, but allows for a certain amount of distance between the narrator and the events. Of course, the dramatic verisimilitude is broken at various places when the author(s) wishes the reader to forget that there is a narrator, yet the dialogue is effective at constructing Des Grieux as a character. Though he does love women, Des Grieux also admits to realizing at a young age that he also loves men. As his interior landscape is the one we get to know, it is also the one that throws over the novel an intense interest in understanding what it means for one man to love—or at least lust after—another.

The book's implicit—and at times explicit—grappling with the question of male homoerotic desire does not always lead to what we might think of as a protogay identity. Indeed, as with *The Hundred Stories*, the interchanging of body parts and genders suggests that one cannot draw lines that are stable. Sexual desire cannot, in other words, be channeled toward one sex, one class, or one act or set of acts that should be grouped together as natural. The licentiousness of *The Hundred Stories* is ultimately of a moral kind that has social meaning and, often, specifically legal consequences, though the fun of manipulating the rules of sex can be had by anyone. In *Teleny*, the adventures of two young men result in the suicide of the maid and the possible loss of a relationship with a beautiful young woman by Des Grieux late in the book, yet the novel's representation of sex does not always seem to reference a fixed moral schema. That is, some of the social, ethical, and even moral ideologies the book encodes exist outside the story— in the community of men who wrote it, in the society in which they perhaps led double lives, in the biographies and autobiographies of famous men.

This difference does not mean, however, that *Teleny*'s premise is that men will one day have an identity or a place within society as "men loving men" but that sexuality is not only a traceable function of sub-culture but also a highly unstable and contingent product of cultural production—especially as inflected through gender and, to a lesser ex-tent, nationality. Like Pasolini's Trilogy of Life—*The Decameron* (1970), *The Canterbury Tales* (1971), and *The Arabian Nights* (1974)—the tales in *The Hundred Stories* are ribald and earthy and promote an attitude toward sex that makes it clear that who one sleeps with is not as impor-tant as how sex is seen as an appetite or an activity that lacks a signifier, and certainly an identity (though Pasolini manages to apply a gay tinge to much of the sex that he represents). Although one should not claim that there is a lack of subjectivity on the part of the characters—or authors—of *The Hundred Stories*, one likewise should not read the rep-resentation of sex and sexuality in them as a utopian space in which there are fewer restrictions on the deployment of power than on mod-ern sexualities. However, it may be possible to argue that a plurality of sexual protodefinitions may have existed before the redefinition of sexu-ality that took place after Wilde's conviction and that became no longer available as a result. Indeed, in *Teleny*, the very ease with which sex seems to be unmoored from any ethical system and to transcend modern boundaries that attempt to keep it reined in connects it to the pansexu-ality of premodern classics such as *The Hundred Stories*. The orgy scene that Des Grieux refers to as "a symposium," for example, is striking in its depiction of sex between men—especially the "climax" with a broken bottle—but also for the ways in which group sex seems carefully delin-eated to create a catalog of sexual acts in which, though privileging male-male sexual acts, still retains an emphasis on the ability for a man to sleep almost equally with men and with women.[41] Indeed, like *The*

Hundred Stories, the mixing of sexes, the ability to exchange one for the other, is in many ways at the heart of the book's "philosophy."

Teleny is not the only book depicting sexual practices to which Wilde was connected. Though he was rumored to be the author of "The Priest and the Acolyte," which appeared in the first number of the *Chameleon*, the actual author was John Francis Bloxam.[42] The attribution of Wilde in this case was probably made for homophobic reasons and was perhaps suggested by the fact that he published "Phrases and Philosophies" anonymously in the same issue. More significantly, Wilde was connected to a translation of the *Satyricon of Petronius* in a private edition printed and reprinted at various times.[43] In yet another book filled with both same-sex and cross-sex attraction, the queer space Wilde attempted to open up for the next century may well have been an alternative model to the homo/hetero binary of the twentieth and twenty-first centuries. That is, naming "Wilde" may have signified a space alternate to the one of gay versus straight given to it by Koestenbaum but questioned by Sinfield. Wilde's name, in other words, might have signified not the emergence of a new type that would today be thought of as gay; rather, his identity, whether borrowed for *Teleny* or given to it pseudonymously by him, may have established a space for the exploration of sexual queerness—a place to queer the straight—that was either lost after the verdict of his trial or, more likely, suppressed in favor of the medical or anticultural definitions that came to dominate (and still do) after his imprisonment.

The connection of Wilde to *Teleny* and to the anonymous translation of the *Satyricon* points to a matrix of associations that existed at the time Wilde was writing in which the "Oriental" structure of *The Arabian Nights*—with its stories of various sexual exploits—could be crossed with something like the medieval *Cents Nouvelles* and *The Decameron* to produce a text like *Teleny*.[44] In Wilde's own tendencies to privilege the Oriental in his writing—praising the minimalism of Japanese style and the subtlety of Chinese philosophy, for example—he consistently linked the Asian with the polyglot and the vaguely unnamable: a region of knowledge that was not known to the common man. Just as Dorian's homosexuality is named only by reference to opium eating, *Teleny*'s primary signifier is a reference to an arcane short story whose name is itself a signifier of sexual "excess."[45] The esoteric and pornographic reputation of *The Hundred Stories* places it within a tradition of canonical texts, like the *Kama-sutra*, that are known to possess some secret knowledge about sex and sexuality by linking the Oriental with the pornographic.[46]

Like *Les Cent Nouvelles*, the structure of *Teleny* is also much like Sade's *120 Days of Sodom*: a day for each sexual act—or actor—and a story for each evening's entertainment. The multitale form allows for a continuous stream of new characters, plots, sexual acts, and, possibly, authors and contributors. And like the tales of the Marquis de Sade, the book's structure mirrors a sense of the endlessness of pleasure—a series of nights (stories) that will never end or a serial pleasure that, in the age of advertising, cigarettes, and other new forms of stimulus, would seem the most "natural" form imaginable: the commodity.[47] If Wilde coordinated the production of *Teleny*, what he did was to harness this structure to a narrative that, in its being told as a putative dialogue, makes the reader into an audience to one evening's long story of several "adventures" had by the narrator and his friend. Wilde is able, therefore, to link the structure of the collection of tales—the original romance structure—to the more recent romantic structure of the polysemous experimental novel.[48] The editor of *Teleny* took the German romantic idea one step further and created a work whose multiple voices actually come from multiple people. Like the *Athenaeum*, *Teleny* is a collective effort in which fragments have been put together to form a whole that functions as a novel even as it questions what a novel might be. The authors create, in other words, a medieval romance, not a novel—or, rather, a novel as Schlegel defined it.[49]

That Wilde's ideas and general language are either present or mimicked in *Teleny* is obvious; whether he is its author is more difficult to tell. It is certain, however, that the milieu that is depicted there is one that is named for him if not explicitly by him, and that the power of his "type" provided a potent legacy that would not soon dissipate in the next century. In fact, Wilde's "type" might simply have been the distillation of one particular strain of queer identity that was active at the time. Wilde's trial, then, was to a large extent about the making visible of a community activity—men sleeping with men—as it was practiced by the upper-class male culture of the time. In this sense, Wilde was a scapegoat for indiscretion—or, of course, blackmail. *Teleny* may be seen to mirror this community and culture of (mostly) closeted men who enjoyed each other as well as younger working-class men for a fee. Indeed, it was Lord Alfred, not Robbie Ross, who introduced Wilde to "trade." *Teleny* places Wilde's own sexuality within a framework that was established around him and in which he became a willing participant— probably as early as Oxford—until he was undone by the paranoid but powerful agents of the class to which he had aspired. To attribute *Teleny* to Wilde is therefore to admit that he was aware of the double life that an artist and/or aristocrat might lead in late Victorian London—one in which a man becomes part of a community of young men who share a similar interest. The prisoners of *Reading Gaol* are a later community: one that is the very obverse of the community of which Wilde at one time felt himself a part. The members of the coterie that composed *Teleny*—like the larger one that later read it—are a part of the same cultural matrix that defined British social and political power well into the next century.

By linking *Teleny* to *The Hundred Stories*, the editor was also acknowledging the allusions in the novel's structure to Baccaccio and Rabelais, but also to late Victorian sensations such as Burton's *Arabian Nights*. Indeed, what figure best exemplifies the complexity and contradiction of the group to which Wilde aspired than Burton? A cross-dressing explorer who discovered the source of the Nile (while accompanied by his close friend Speke), Burton went on to translate the *Kama-sutra*. Always claiming the privilege of seeming straight, he mainly succeeded in seeming butch: the gay deconstruction of masculinity as a norm. A Byronic figure for the late nineteenth century, his sixteen-volume translation of the *Arabian Nights* (1885 until his death in 1890), which was in itself a major scholarly achievement, not only was a possible model for *Teleny* but was, in the "Terminal Essay" (1890), one of the few works to discuss same-sex male activity explicitly.[50] Probably written as a response to Symonds's *A Problem in Greek Ethics* (1883),[51] the "Terminal Essay" is a treatise that in fact confuses the categories of its own putative subject. Often simply referring to pederasty as "Le Vice," Burton never seems able to name what he is discussing.

Burton begins with a description of male bordellos, only to switch to a discussion of sodomy as a practice, and finally to slip completely away from any stable structure as he begins a long catalog of names. Indeed, Burton seems so unable to label what he wants to talk about that he ends up naming it over and over again. Burton's fifty-seven-page typescript in fact becomes a sort of Damron's guide for the late-nineteenth-century "gay" man as Burton desperately attempts to define his concept of the "Sotadic Zone"—an asymmetrical region of the Earth roughly bounding the Mediterranean in Europe before swelling out to embrace all of "Asia Minor, Mesopotamia, Chaldaea, Afghanistan, Sind, the Punjab, and Kashmir," as well as "China, Japan and Turkistan" and "the South Sea Islands and the New World."[52] Leaving little out except northern Europe, Burton's "essay" lists every example of the vice that he has ever been able to uncover either by historical research, literary reference, word of mouth, or faithful observation. Indeed, Burton so obsesses on creating shadings and fine distinctions between versions of male homosexuality—the Persians do it because of "parental severity" and the Chinese because they are bestial—that he names and renames "pederasty" in his translations and transliterations of the work from dozens of languages. He sets up categories for making the distinctions that seem important to him, even though he must frequently resort to Latin out of a putative sense of decorum. A master of twenty-three languages and dialects, Burton creates a topography of male-male sexual practice that ultimately links men by the very universality of this one unnamable activity/desire/identity. His essay stands alongside *Teleny* as another example of the heterogeneity of what may now be called male homosexual panic, but which was then simply called culture. Not only is *Teleny*'s structure similar to the tales of *The Thousand Nights and a Night*, but its thesis is laid out by Burton in the essay he stuck to the end of his translation—an ending that, unlike the wife's backside, identifies all.[53]

At the beginning of his essay, Burton gives a definition of "the pathic" as someone in whom "the nerves of the rectum and the genitalia, in all cases closely connected, are abnormally so . . . [and] who obtains, by intromission, the venereal orgasm which is usually sought through the sexual organs." Burton uses a woman to illustrate this definition—specifically a lesbian, which he designates by using one of the terms of classification popular at the time, "tribad": "So amongst women there are tribads who can procure no pleasure except by foreign objects introduced a posteriori." Why Burton uses a woman's body as the signifying instance of anal eroticism in this essay is never completely clear, but this is the only example in the essay of what Burton means by the physical act that he is constantly referencing on different scales.[54] Indeed, even this anatomical definition is really set up only to be summarily dismissed a couple of sentences later when Burton states his thesis: the explanation for sodomy cannot be found in the body or in the mind—as many have argued—but only in "the manifold subtle influences massed together in the word climate."[55] Only a general concept, in other words, can explain so broad—so pervasive—a phenomenon. Burton attempts to map homosexuality, only to find that by spatializing all known types, in the end, he only knows that he cannot explain them because the very plurality so endangers the category that anything beyond mere description creates epistemological problems that multiply at a geometric rate.[56]

Burton bases his nomenclature not only on geographic distribution but also on historical and literary data. Along this axis, Burton links male-male desire through the ages—often collapsing the category of literary reference with contemporary "documented" ones by allowing the former to act as proof for practices that he assumes must continue into the present. As part of this temporal designation, he references both France in the sixteenth century, which "had four hundred names for the parts genital and three hundred for their use in coition,"[57] and, on two separate occasions, the creation of an entire series of definitions of pederasty in the *Satyricon*.[58] As Symonds later pointed out in an essay published as an afterword, Burton's classification of pederasty into three categories hardly covers the known instances and does not really explain its prevalence or even its existence as a practice.[59] Indeed, by comparing the ways in which pederasts know one another by their secret hand-shakes, "like the freemasons,"[60] Burton accidentally hints that he does think that pederasty exists in northern Europe, even though he denies calling this part of the world a place where pederasty is natural—unlike his Sotadic Zone—because of the climate.[61] In fact, Symonds points out the absurdity of denying this classification—of not acknowledging its aptness—for northern Europe. Indeed, the sheer number of examples that make up the essay belie his two or three feeble denials of any inter-est in the activity. Yet it is important to note that what Burton actu-ally claims is that an Englishman would be "much scandalised by being called Gand-mara (anus beater) or Ganda (anuser)"—Hindi words for the equivalent of whatever Burton is trying to name.[62] It is the name—the type for which a name must be found—that Burton cannot find (or finds too much of).

Burton's essay ends with a polemical argument against censor-ship in which he wonders why it is not hypocritical to "mourn over the 'Pornography' of *The Nights*, dwell upon the 'ethics of dirt' and the 'Gar-bage of the Brothel,'" and yet read "Aristophones, and Plato, Horace and Virgil" and require boys and young men to study "Boccaccio and Chaucer, Shakespeare and Rabelais, [and] Burton" in complete editions at school.[63] Burton places himself not only within the canon of great literature but also among those figures who have not been afraid to represent sexual acts—including homoerotic ones—in their work. Many of these figures were themselves, of course, of either undetermined or at least changeable sexuality. In a note to the essay, Burton reproduces a "list of famous pederasts," which includes Alexander, Caesar, Napoleon, Henry III, Louis XIII and Louis XVIII of France, Frederick II of Prus-sia, and Peter the Great. Shakespeare is listed again, along with Molière, Sainte-Beuve, and an entire phalanx of notable French figures.[64] Burton's self-conscious interpellation of himself into history—his self-invention as an explorer and an Orientalist—includes placing himself at the center of the study of, the exploration of, male same-sex definition at the crucial point in medical and legal history when in Germany, France, and England, Symonds, Ellis, Ulrichs, and others were attempting to define "inversion." However, as Symonds notes, rather than trying "to conjecture" that pederasty "takes place universally," it might be more "philosophical"—that is, sensible—to explore "the consequences" that pederasty is "only tolerated in certain parts of the globe."[65] That is, the Sotadic Zone is merely a zone of all or partial tolerance, while the "vice" is always already everywhere. Burton, in his own odd way, helps to make visible that which cannot be named without, however, understanding that the problem is a political one that has little to do with climate or the name, for that matter, by which it is identified.

In his 1885 introduction to the *Nights*, Burton says that explanations for his translations will be found in the "Terminal Essay." These explanations are not, however, at all apparent in the essay Burton ultimately wrote. The work that he imagines that essay as doing is, in other words, not what he implies that it is doing in a literal sense, though it is all about translation in many other senses. Importantly, Burton's essay is left out of the popular version of the translation, thereby denying the majority of readers that which Burton himself thought to be the key to how to read the work as a whole. Just as "The Reverse of the Medal" provides the key to the editor of *Teleny*—or, at least, to the meaning of the novel's structure—so too was "The Sotadic Zone," as the essay was later renamed when reprinted in the United States, supposed to provide the literal key to Burton's opus. "Sotadic," as the *OED* defines it, has as one of its definitions "Capable of being read in reverse order; palindrome." The "Terminal Essay" can indeed be read first and, like *Teleny*, provides a key to the whole enterprise. Likewise, *Teleny*, the reverse of *Dorian Gray*, may in fact be its front side: the hidden part that, when uncovered, merely tells the truth through a deception whose meaning is known to whoever is in the know.

CHAPTER 3

Performing Wilde

Mechanical Bodies and Desiring Machines:
The Importance of Being Earnest

> *I* will survive; I'm my finest work of art.
>
> —Terry Eagleton, *Saint Oscar*

Wilde's interest in the typing and printing of the work he wrote while in prison shows his interest in the mechanical striking of (a) type. As Wayne Koestenbaum notes, Wilde wanted *De Profundis* to be set down with a typewriter as soon as possible, specifying "that Ross 'must read it carefully and *copy it out carefully every word* for me.'"[1] Even though he had produced what was nominally a personal letter, he knew that its permanence—and perhaps modernity—could only be ensured through typewriting. Whether or not Wilde preferred his own new type—the type of the proto-gay man—is perhaps uncertain, as he was given little choice in the matter. What is clear is that Wilde, by the twentieth century's definition, came out of the closet. After his release from prison, Richard Ellmann recounts that "Wilde lolled about with young men. As he wrote to Smithers, 'Yes: even at Napoule there is romance: it comes in boats, and takes the form of fisher-lads, who draw great nets, and are bare-limbed: they are strangely perfect.'" During this stay, Wilde considered writing a "counterstatement to *The Ballad of Reading Gaol*, which he planned to call 'The Ballad of the Fisher Boy.' He would celebrate liberty instead of prison, joy instead of hanging. The three stanzas he quoted from the unwritten poem were not unpromising, and Harris urged him to write them down. Wilde refused. He could write no more."[2] Wilde was unable to write again, and did not, so far as we know, though he was perhaps finally ready to write about what had always been the subject of his work—namely, the "strangely perfect" beauty of young men. Yet at the brink of this writing—the work that would be the most like *Teleny*, perhaps—Wilde was unable to go beyond the type he had been made into, to celebrate it in an open way.

Had Wilde lived on unaffected by the penal system, it is likely that he would have acknowledged the alignment of certain characteristics of homocentric male identity into something new, but it is not as likely that he would have given his own name to it, as this identity—ultimately imposed on him—was not the type he was developing at the time of his trials. The legacy of Wilde—like Wilde's inheritance—has been too narrowly tied to a redefinition of sexuality as a bipolar experience. If *Teleny* is an indicator of where he was headed in his own thinking about sex and gender, then it was toward what we could perhaps best describe as a Deleuzian matrix of desire in which the ascription of sex was clearly a social construction rather than in any way an answer to the questions generated about sex in the next century.[3] Like Deleuze and Guattari's, Wilde's symbols for sex were mechanistic ones—German romantic arabesques and "wire-pulled automatons"—images he used not only in "The Harlot's House" and in *Dorian Gray* but also in *Reading Gaol*. For Wilde, the solution to escaping the proscriptions placed on one by the state apparatus was to proliferate sexualities, or, in Deleuzian terms, to become a "plane of consistency," to conclude, that is, as *Teleny* does, with an attempt to represent multiplicity as integral to sexuality.

Wilde and Pater were both known to support an "aesthetic cult of dead bodies" that must certainly have been based on Baudelaire's symbolism and perhaps the popular fad of the period for photographing the dead.[4] Wilde's use of the medieval *danse macabre* in "The Harlot's

House" is a modern update of the "ashes to ashes" motif on which it is based. In chapter 16 of *Dorian Gray*, Wilde reproduces a prose version of his famous poem:

> After some time they left the clay road, and rattled again over rough-paven streets. Most of the windows were dark, but now and then fantastic shadows were silhouetted against some lamp-lit blind. He [Dorian] watched them curiously. They moved liked monstrous marionettes, and made gestures like live things. He hated them. . . . [T]wo men ran after the hansom. . . . The driver beat them with his whip. It is said that passion makes one think in a circle.[5]

This description of the mechanical aspect of desire appears again in *Gaol* when, in the third section, "evil sprite[s]" "seemed to play" in a dance:

> They trod a saraband:
> And the damned grotesques made arabesques,
> Like the wind upon the sand!
>
> With the pirouettes of marionettes
> They tripped on pointed tread:
> But with flutes of Fear they filled the ear,
> As their grisly masque they led,
> And loud they sang . . .
> For they sang to wake the dead.[6]

The spirits here—presumably former condemned men, but also abstract symbols of terror—appear for the atmospheric purposes of the poem's melodramatics—specifically, the foreshadowing of the hanging to come. In the earlier incarnations, however, the "mechanical grotesques" denote what happens when love turns into lust. In "The Harlot's House," the speaker's companion is tempted inside, which begins a kind of entropy:

But she—she heard the violin,
And left my side, and entered in:
Love passed into the house of lust.

Then suddenly the tune went false,
The dancers wearied of the waltz
The shadows ceased to wheel and whirl.[7]

The speaker's actual lover—and allegorically love itself—passes from one reality into another, causing a transformation of romantic love into sexual lust. Wilde's point is that love ceases to be living and creative when it becomes simply lustful and mechanical. As he says in "The Critic as Artist": "When man acts he is a puppet. When he describes he is a poet."[8]

Though one might psychologize Wilde's poem and see it as connected to his fear of syphilis, which he supposedly contracted from a female prostitute while he was a student at Oxford, it seems more likely that it is an indictment of the reduction of sexuality to coitus, an act that Wilde apparently did not mind but also did not particularly cathect onto, either. The problem with this reading is that Wilde makes the harlot's house so very attractive: there is a party going on, and the meter of the poem—set to waltz time—uses every bit of sound, image, and aspiration to create the dance atmosphere and to conjure the clocklike mechanics the poem describes. Though perhaps this precision is meant to be off-putting on one level—it is just too perfect—it is also what draws the reader in. The poem's ability to find the perfect match of sound and image is infectious. Therefore the ending of the poem, though dramatic, is inevitably a letdown: "The dawn, with silver-sandalled feet, / Crept like a frightened girl." Indeed, is this what happens to the "she" of the poem? Or is the bathetic image supposed to suggest only the classical allegory of the dawn as a young girl? It is difficult to say, just as it is not easy to determine whether the poem is a comment on heterosexual prostitution or a kind of warning by the author to himself that dabbling in the homoerotic is acceptable so long as it is kept pure and

Platonic, but a problem as soon as it becomes physical. By reproducing the poem's images in the particular section of *Dorian Gray* that he does, Wilde seems to want to make sure that readers not miss the association of the poem with the distinctly proto-gay milieu of the infamous black-mailing scene with Alan Singleton. Within this context, it is difficult not to see the poem as autobiographical: Wilde and a friend—most likely male and young—stop by a house party only to have it break up at dawn, when Wilde must return to his other world. "She," therefore, is most probably "he," and even "love" may in fact be "lust," as the poem inverts its meanings in an attempt—as in *Dorian*—to tell one thing by saying its opposite, to present in a "picture" that which is not shown on the face of the text.

Wilde's most complex and famous use of this type of reversal is in *The Importance of Being Earnest*, which also has associations with mechanical bodies. As Eve Kosofsky Sedgwick points out, all the characters in the play talk as though they were genderless automatons whose witty dialogue appears in their heads not only effortlessly but as if it were being fed to them by a puppet master.[9] Indeed, the bodies represented by Wilde seem almost devoid of adult passion, functioning like futuristic children for whom wit and subversion come as easily as prudery and ingrained hierarchy did to the Victorians in the audience with whom Wilde toyed. The mechanical desiring machines that he imagines in *Earnest* are hardly the semihuman creatures that descend around Dorian's carriage; however, Wilde's shift from "grotesques" to characters such as Gwendolen and Cecily marks a complexifying of his concepts in which he begins to project a possible alternative to the sex/gender system in which he finds himself and his work trapped. The best way to describe the change may be to say that Wilde's concept of the body—or of sexuality itself—moves from a thinking of the body as enmeshed in social systems (whether the satire of the three social comedies or the moralistic conclusion of *Dorian Gray*) toward the creation of a world in which the social is held in abeyance to the individual. That is, Wilde was in the process of suggesting a theoretical model for the deconstruction of the very forces that would rise up—in all the terrible strength of the state and mass opinion—to literally enchain him after the trials. The re-working of desire in *Earnest*, therefore, is the creation of an entirely new race of beings perhaps comparable only to those envisioned by Monique Wittig in her creative writing or by Deleuze and Guattari in the concept of the "body without organs" that they develop in *Capitalism and Schizophrenia*.[10]

Deleuze and Guattari provide a critique of Freud that sees the concept of the Oedipus complex as an attempt to regulate desire and take away options by coding the body through the Oedipal drama. The body without organs is a body that is freed from this system—one that they often compare to capitalism—to think desire anew. For Deleuze and Guattari, desire functions within the unconscious mind as a machine or a factory. For them, the danger in Freud's tripartite model of the mind is "the reduction of the factories of the unconscious to a piece of theater. Oedipus or Hamlet."[11] In modeling desire on machines, they "reject . . . all talk of a conflict between man and machine" to say instead "that there's never anything like enough consumption, never anything like enough contrivance: people's interests will never turn in favor of revolution until lines of desire reach the point where desire and machine become indistinguishable, where desire and contrivance are the same thing, turning against the so-called natural principles of, for example, capitalist society" (19–20).

Structures that territorialize desire, such as psychoanalysis, function much like capital. Both are "immanent systems" that constantly overcome their own limitations, only to come "up against them once more in a broader form" (171). For Deleuze and Guattari, a society "is defined not so much by its contradictions as by its lines of flight" (171), by which they mean "lines of absolute decoding" (22). These lines are often represented as rhizomes—lines running underground, beneath the arboreal structures above. In addition to offering the possibility of decoding, rhizomes represent the authors' belief that "there are not universals, only singularities" (146). Similarly, they refuse to see the difference between a minority and the majority as one based on size, since "[a] minority may be bigger than a majority." That is, since the minority is "a becoming, a process" that "has no model," it "creates models for itself" (173). One such minority could be homosexuality—or queerness—especially as imagined by Wilde.

The characters in *Earnest* seem already to have begun the process of making themselves into desiring machines. With their food fights at tea and arguments over cucumber sandwiches, the orality and general pleasure that they have in talking, eating, smoking, and reading aloud can be seen as an attempt on Wilde's part to recode the body.[12] The existence of the name of the father in the war records in the last scene of *Earnest* places Wilde with Deleuze and Guattari against the "abstract machines" that the state uses to control one's body. Wilde plays with the idea that it is only in the war records that Lady Bracknell can find the name of her sister's dead husband—and thus the name of "Ernest"— an episode that is preceded by the attempt of both male leads to be christened "Ernest" in order to marry their female counterparts. The church and the state are brought into alignment to allow for sex—and sexuality. The name of the father in particular corresponds with the law of the father of the Oedipus complex and places the discovery of the name "Ernest" at the center of the three institutions that Deleuze and Guattari would say work in tandem: the state, religion, and psychology. Wilde parodies this alignment in myriad ways—from the fact that Ernest is lost as a child by being mistaken for a novel in a handbag to other surreal moments of mixed, confused, or forgotten identities on the part of Jack and Algy. Gwendolen and Cecily, for their parts, are always in control and make their ability to function as marionettes most clear when they marshal their forces against the men and speak simultaneously in a clocklike rhythm. They, after all, know what they want, and it is up to the men to search for an identity that will please them.[13]

The machinic aspect of the play—the state, religion—is not merely a metaphor for patriarchy (or "familialism," as Sedgwick terms its successor) but is also tied to the concept of the "desiring machine" used by Guy Hocquenghem in *Homosexual Desire*. For Hocquenghem, the theory of polymorphic perversity that Freud wished to substitute for the third-sex theory did not last long, for "no sooner had he discovered

the universality of this 'perversion' than he enclosed it, not geographi-
cally but historically, within the Oedipal system."[14] Hocquenghem's
specific historical referent is Freud's psychoanalysis of da Vinci: while
seeming to argue for the ability of homosexual desire to manifest itself
in everyone, the text also sets it up as "neurotic." Hocquenghem's theorizing of homosexual desire therefore includes an attack on what he sees
as the hierarchical nature of heterosexuality—specifically, the necessity
of using the Oedipus myth for the policing and ultimate heterosexual-
ization of all desire. In the leftist political rhetoric with which he infuses
his book, Hocquenghem argues for homosexual desire as the creation of
"a mode of non-limitative horizontal relations" (95). He substitutes for
the Oedipal hierarchy in which "every individual knows that it will one
day be his turn to occupy the place already determined by the triangle"
the image of "the cruising homosexual, on the look-out for anything
that might come and plug in to his own desire" (95, 117). The consequences of this alternative model include the possibility that "to encounter desire is first of all to forget the difference in the sexes" (116),
which he sees happening in Proust—and I would argue occurs to some
extent in *Earnest*—but also that "the sexualisation of the world heralded
by the gay movement pushes capitalist decoding to the limit and corresponds to the dissolution of the human; from this point of view, the gay
movement undertakes the necessary dehumanisation" (131).

Hocquenghem argues that in Proust's famous scene between
Jupien and Charlus in which the third-sex theory is discussed by the
narrator as a model for homosexual desire, the "flowers and insects have
no sex; they are the very *machine* of sexual *desire*" (77). This machine, for
Hocquenghem, is not simply the advent of an Oedipal model—as occurs
later with Freud—but an already-existing state apparatus that comes,
indeed, with the advent of capitalism. The very definition of social relations depends on the phallus; its absence—as in Proust—points to the
absence of sex itself. The anus, in contrast, is the very essence (or signification) of this lack. If the phallus is social, then "the anus must be
privatised in individualised and Oedipalised persons" (82). The anus
represents "sublimation" itself. The coming of this privatization—of the

loss of signification—is the coming of capitalism and its concomitant "progress," as Freud would see it.[15] It is only with Deleuze and Guattari's countermodel that we have "another possible social relation which is not vertical but horizontal."[16] That is, gay men, in their practices and in their ability to create a social countermodel—an alternative desiring machine—provide the praxis for Deleuze and Guattari's theory of anti-Oedipalization. Or, as Hocquenghem argues, "Homosexual desire is . . . the operation of the desiring machine plugged into the anus."[17]

In *Earnest*, then, the play's "imperative" "Forget the Name of the Father!" is Wilde's way of ignoring the phallus—of making its removal from the social relations in the play, from the reality created in the world of the play—all the more pointed. After all, if familial power resides with anyone, it rests on the ample shoulders of Aunt Augusta—frequently a role played (apropos to *Charley's Aunt*) by a man.[18] Phallic power, in other words, does not obey gender roles in this play or, more accurately, does not really exist at all. The play's genius is to present a hunt for the name of this power—the name of "Ernest," or perhaps of "Bunberry," which is the name given here to privatized anality. Indeed, the uniqueness of Bunberry—a relative/ruse belonging to Jack that he is only too happy, however, to share—is an activity that, by the play's end, turns out to be the very basis of most of the relationships the play recounts. That is, by the end, it turns out that almost everyone has been Bunberrying or, at the very least, has been engaged in an individualized version of the same.

As Sedgwick notes, the play actually sets up an alternative definition of the Oedipal family—one composed of "aunts" and "uncles"—that disrupts the capitalist definition of family by creating "diagonal" relationships that supplant the "biological" definition with "an avuncular function."[19] This structure is part of the play's ability to trace a change in society in which "the precapitalist or early-capitalist functions of the Name of the Father [have] been substantially superseded, in a process accelerating the Name of the Family—that is, the name Family."[20] That is, *Earnest* represents and replays with amazing repetition the failure of this representation. The same strategy called for by Hocquenghem—

CHAPTER 2

Attributing Wilde

Wilde as "Type"

What is the general type of your build—heavy or slight, muscular or
not robust, fat or thin, tall or short (for your sex) in stature?

—Neil Bartlett

Although Wilde was aware of his connection to the past—the Hellenism and romance that were once again alive in his day—his acute
sense of the modern often took the form of a desire to create something
that was available for the first time to him and those who would follow
him. Wilde's desire to create something new has been described as a
bewildering series of beliefs that changed with each new persona that
he donned, as the putting on of various fashionable ideas belonging to
others (Arnold, Pater, Whistler), or as the subtle "maturing" of a talent
away from theatricality and toward genuine art. In each of these cases,
however, the telos is the same: Wilde's life ends when he becomes
involved with a gay subculture. In these scenarios it is assumed that
De Profundis and *The Ballad of Reading Gaol* are simply the mannered
or sentimental leftovers from a career that—ending more or less with
Earnest—was at the brink of becoming something substantial. What
this other phase would have been is never quite clear. What is known
is that Wilde himself considered *An Ideal Husband* to be his best play,

23

and found by him in the burgeoning gay rights movement of the early 1970s in Europe and North America at the time of his writing—was the one identified by Wilde in his play: show the phallus for what it really is and free the anus. Or, as he says, "desire is at first a universally distributed set of diverse and non-exclusive drives, of erotisms based on the plugging in of organs according to the 'and/and' rather than the 'either/or' mode."[21] Wilde's play, with its reconstruction of the body as a constantly eating, talking, desiring machine, was simply expressing the Freudian pre-Oedipal stage as not only a superior one but also the most sophisticated version of what we might imagine for ourselves when taken to another level altogether. By representing these "machines" as childlike, Wilde was able to represent homosexuality the way it was imagined by society. As Hocquenghem notes, "Homosexuality is reduced to non-sexuality because real sexuality is the sexuality of identifiable persons, of the Oedipus complex" (134). That is, the puppets in Wilde's world appear at first to be the sexless children of Oedipus, but they turn out to be the types of a new expression of the desire that Wilde—like many others—was in the process of attempting to name.

Like any other Victorian play, *The Importance of Being Earnest* seems to ignore homosexual desire, yet by constructing the play around figures who seem to be extreme versions of heterosexual desire—and denial— Wilde actually calls attention to the presence of homosexuality (or, more accurately, queerness) everywhere. The location of the name of the father in the military—with the help of the church and the family—is exactly where Deleuze and Guattari would locate the most stultifying examples of machines that would shut down desire. As Hocquenghem suggests:

> The latent homosexuality so beloved by psychoanalysts corresponds to the oppression of patent homosexuality; and we find the greatest charge of latent homosexuality in those social machines which are particularly anti-homosexual—the army, the school, the church, sport, etc. At the collective level, this sublimation is a means of transforming desire into the desire to repress. (58)

Freud's theories, therefore, are simply the "internal barriers" that arise when external barriers—what we could perhaps now recognize as late capitalism—begin to dissolve. Freud "is both the discoverer of the mechanisms of desire and the organiser of their control" (59). Wilde, by contrast, not only recognizes many of the same mechanisms of desire but also attempts—like Deleuze and Wittig much later—to offer what they would call "lines of flight" away from the abstract machines that would attempt not only to stifle desire's multiplicity but to resurrect new regimes of control.

The only way out, as Wilde made clear, was through a new definition of the body and a new form with which to represent it. For Wilde, therefore, the putative homosexual type is not so much an identity in a binary relationship with heterosexuality as it is an emerging practice or activity that carries with it the possibility of the radical subversion of meaning as it is constituted in social and literary mores. The blending of sexuality into everything was an attempt not to make the world aesthetic (Wilde's earlier goal) but to make the world queer in the sense that all actions could be seen not as either right or wrong but rather as either successful or not at effectuating the result most—and most often—desired. In this sense, then, *Earnest* is a performance about performance, as it is only by performing a gender—or a sexuality—via the use of masks and language that one can begin to manipulate and change the status quo. As Jean Genet would later do, Wilde raises questions about what exactly is being performed by characters onstage—and, by extension, people off the stage. If, in his effeminacy, Wilde was himself performing a different gender, then he was also attempting to perform other roles as well. In *Earnest*, the template for this type of total art form—a blending of the personal with the objective that he adamantly desired—results in a creation that replays what he had learned about the performance of self. Or rather, the play is the perfect expression of everything that Wilde could teach about his ability to express himself in a form that could be performed by others.

In addition to being a play about the mechanics of desire, therefore, the play itself functions like a machine—one in which the performers

must act their roles with absolute sincerity in order for the characteri-
zations to work. Wilde's play is famous for its infallibility as comedy.
The power of the play's automatics does not mean, however, that the
characters in the play exist as types. Wilde's work had become too complex for so simple a correspondence. The play, like the postprison work,
has a typological function only to the extent to which it acts as an
expression of Wilde's own interest in discovering the possibilities in
himself. If *Dorian Gray* represented—in the characters of Basil, Harry,
and Dorian—the splitting of his consciousness into three separate versions of himself, then *Earnest* carries his new self into the arena of pure
concept.[22] It represents a world where queer space is not merely hinted
at but explicitly defined.

As Lawrence Danson has recently written, "Wilde tried to rename
the world in order to avoid for himself the categorizing which makes us
exemplars of the already constructed."[23] All Wilde's critical and creative
writing before prison illustrates this strategy in play. Wilde's project was
similar to Hocquenghem's rejection of identity politics—a refusal even
to sketch a possible praxis, for as soon as one does, one simply resur-
rects the categories themselves. As he argues in *Homosexual Desire*, "In
fact the homosexual 'choice' is only a rationalisation operated by the
Oedipal system, by means of a differentiation among whole people in a
relation of exclusive object-choice."[24] Wilde tries to avoid this problem
in *Earnest* by creating a world within the play in which "nothing stands
in the way of . . . self-creation, for reality itself is infinitely adaptable."[25]
Sos Elitis notes that for most farces of the time,

> comedy derives from increasingly complicated attempts by the charac-
> ters to hide former marriages and affairs, and their real social status. In
> the end the truth is revealed, and the fictitious characters . . . evaporate.
> In *The Importance of Being Earnest*, on the contrary, the characters' fan-
> tasies are brought to life at the end of the play; in its anarchic world
> characters are free to multiply themselves . . . and to live fantasy lives
> without anyone else intervening to insist on the higher authority of the
> truth.[26]

The postprison work, by contrast, represents a world in which the choices that are now available are few, and the type of the homosexual has been defined as not only sentimental but also pathological. What Wilde's sexuality might have suggested if the coming of the homo/hetero divide had not foreshortened it is something that we will obviously never know. In a text like *Earnest*, however, we can see that Wilde rejected simple binaries and posited a version of queer sexuality that is clearly understandable perhaps only now—over one hundred years later—when we have concepts and theories that help us to recognize what he was doing. What might Wilde have become if he were not remade by his trials? To read Wilde as gay rather than queer is to read him retroactively, from the perspective of our time, rather than to attempt to see what sort of future he might have imagined when he still had the chance to do so.

An Erotics of Opportunity: *De Profundis*

> The highest, as the lowest, form of criticism is the autobiography.
>
> —Wilde

The use of conversation in *The Importance of Being Earnest*—the ability to go beyond *Dorian Gray* to experiment successfully with a way to reconfigure the straight world as queer—is transformed in *De Profundis* into a monologue on the dystopic features of self-creation. Wilde continues to develop and meditate on his own performative abilities—on conversation as performance—but his outlet for communication shrinks from the whole of London to the confines of a prison cell. Wilde's abilities at self-promotion, perhaps surprisingly, do not subside, but his approach becomes that of the confessional letter rather than the play. What remains peculiarly Wildean is the fact that he writes the letter—a private letter to a lover—for everyone to read. Indeed, Wilde turns the sentimental genre of the confessional into a presentation of himself as a new public type in which he attempts to redefine himself for the world. That is, he takes on the type of the homosexual but attempts simultaneously to transform it on his own. He tries, in other words, to define his decline and fall for himself—to once again author himself in the midst of what seems like failure. The manner in which Wilde chooses to do this is to combine in one form of writing, the epistle, many of the genres at which he excelled—critique, philosophic argument, history of ideas, and so forth—with genres he had not really explored before in much detail, such as the religious confessional and the sincere auto-biography. *De Profundis*, then, is a literary performance: an attempt to seem contrite, it is at the same time a mode of revenge on the one person, Lord Alfred Douglas, whose youth and self-absorption let Wilde down, but whom he still loves.

Indeed, Wilde's approach to Lord Douglas is to present him with a version of events as he sees them. That is, he uses his powers of argument to create a history of their life together that contains within it a justification of his actions—those that putatively led to his own imprisonment and infamy. Central to his creation of a history alternative to that given in official reports is his admission not only that his relationship with Douglas was a romantic one but that it was also economic. It may seem odd that Wilde would have to provide economic support for Douglas, but in fact, though Douglas was in possession of a title, he refused to be supported by his family while he was with Wilde. Wilde knew that Douglas's estrangement from his father, the Marquess of Queensberry, put their relationship into a precarious position. Knowing better than Douglas the eventual importance of his family's wealth, Wilde tried to persuade him not to sever family ties. Wilde, however, was forced to play not only the part he seemed to enjoy—the decadent older man who is both instructor and lover—but also the surrogate father figure who would entertain Douglas in the style in which he was accustomed. Wilde's extravagance, which probably strongly impressed the "trade" to which Douglas introduced him, was seen by Douglas as merely what he expected—or so Wilde suggests.

Wilde's intense awareness of the price exacted for his time with Douglas—not only the toll on his marriage but also the cost of champagne at Willis's on any particular night—comes out of Wilde's economic mind-set. Wilde's self-invention has everything to do with his own striving after middle-class—and even upper-class—security and, in many ways, pretension.[27] Wilde's economic struggle on coming to London after his North American tour was a real one that taught him much about not only the complexity of building a career but also the necessity of being vigilant about always working toward it. Indeed, for much of his earlier career, Wilde's own class standing would have been that of a borderline professional, which meant he could afford one or two servants, was educated, but was slow to make increases in money. The number of readers for his books, likewise, would have been small. After he was refused a position at Oxford, his economic instability and attempts to be successful as a freelance writer placed him in a precarious financial situation. Much of what we might see as Wilde's extravagance—his elaborate decorations for his home and clothing for himself and his wife—was an attempt to popularize himself as an arbiter of taste: to create a Wildean style. Lessons he learned on his North American tour—that the public buys the image, not the speech—were transformed in the fertile arena of English consumer society into an attempt on his part to mount a synergistic campaign to refract his tastes and attentions through as many different projects, venues, and products as possible. Wilde's self-invention, in other words, was a constant media blitz.

The form that Wilde's self-publicity would first take in London was as the new editor of a general-interest magazine entitled *The Lady's World*, which Wilde was to transform by introducing not only topics that were at the time considered of little interest to the average woman because of their intellectual nature but also by renaming the publication *The Woman's World* and completely redesigning its visual look—including its layout and use of models.[28] Indeed, Wilde's first attempt to create his own economic enterprise raises important questions about the relationship between Wilde's sexuality and gender. Though this is a realm that has received some treatment by Ed Cohen, Alan Sinfield, and Joseph Bristow in recent books on Wilde, there is much that still needs to be said about Wilde's relationship to the "New Woman" and how his economic insecurity forced him to attempt to establish a career using the options available to a woman of the time: namely, charm, conversation, and the performance of an interesting self. Wilde, in other words, pursued the path available to women of his class standing—and, indeed, he somewhat deconstructed it as he organized his career around a trajectory that emphasized posing, visibility, and social expertise.

Far from acting like an aesthete who was removed from the dreary concerns of running a business, Wilde worked around the clock on almost every aspect of creating, producing, and selling the publication to the public. As Ian Small argues in an essay on Wilde's professionalism, Wilde knew that it was up to him to create excitement for the magazine and to garner the support of women who were arbiters of fashion. In other words, Wilde was associating his magazine with people whose names would sell the publication by creating an image for it in the public's mind.[29] Wilde's shrewdness at doing business, however, was backed up by the sheer amount of hard work he put into its promotion. Wilde seems to have understood that the magazine would be successful only if it was perceived as successful—a point probably learned in part through the exertions of creating himself and his own career as a litterateur.[30] Douglas's father had accused Wilde of "posing as a somdomite [sic]," yet he did not think that Wilde was one—but merely acted as one might act. For Wilde, poses were not about pretending to be something that he was not. Rather, Wilde posed as that which he wished most to be. This elaborate performance reflected a material realization that to be something, you must first create the illusion of its existence. To paraphrase Wilde in another context, it is only when opinion begins to be set about something that it begins to exist—and at that point, the true artist moves on.

Yet as Small notes, the portrait of Wilde often painted by his best biographers—including Richard Ellmann—is in part inaccurate in its portrayal of Wilde as a social animal whose life consisted only of a series of society dinners. Wilde's public performances out on the town with his wife, Constance Lloyd, and later Douglas, were a form of work, as well. Indeed, Wilde's performance as various types was part of his success at "marketing." Of course, Wilde excelled at conversation, but one might also say that Wilde's self-promotion was for a specific reason—to secure a book deal, obtain a new patron, or make a good impression on a publisher.[31] That is, he was doing this aspect of his job well. What this meant was that Wilde invested his persona with authority. In his critical dialogues and letters in response to his critics, Wilde argued for a form of subjective criticism that placed authority in the speaker, rather than in what was said. Wilde's performative abilities, in other words, not only helped to put him in a situation where he could shine for the purposes of networking for his projects but went further to transform conversation into an opportunity to use autobiography and self-promotion to entice the public into buying either his image of himself or the one he helped to create by playing into the hands of the media—even when the image was a somewhat negative or inaccurate version of himself.[32]

This process was, of course, somewhat dangerous. As Small observes, by shifting the emphasis from the argument to the one who argues, Wilde and Pater may have called forth the ad hominem attacks from reviewers that met *Dorian Gray* and *The Renaissance*, respectively—attacks that not only criticized the former as inartistic and the latter as unscholarly but were bold in their accusations of homosexuality. Though Small's criticism does not explain why other gay men also met similar attacks, he is correct in noting that Wilde's radical critiques of the establishment—ones that I would claim came as much from his career path as his radical ideas themselves—resulted in a circular situation in which reviewers of Wilde and Pater, by criticizing them personally, simply reproduced the very weakening of Victorian cultural authority begun by Wilde's and Pater's work. The shifting of emphasis away from cultural authority as argument and toward the cultural or performative capital of the speaker dissolved the boundary between the author as a maker of a text or work and the author as one who performs a position or a style. Wilde's subversive abilities as an instigator of radical ideas were tied to his ability to function as a changeable type: as a figment of style that was, in reality, a barometer of the market.[33]

To see Wilde at work in his capacity as a performer of himself, one can of course extrapolate from his criticism, plays, and selected scenes

in his fiction. However, firsthand accounts of his conversational skills—
especially interviews—provide a useful illustration of his own performative style in public; that is, one can see that his manner of speaking,
gesturing, and other aspects of what one may identify as the many com-
ponents that make up his performance of self were highly self-conscious.
Although much was written about Wilde's changing styles of dress—
from velveteen suits and long hair, to fashionably conservative clothing
and a Nero bob, to the rather nondescript yet still carefully thought-
out wardrobe of his Continental exile—his manner of speaking was considered equally impressive. In an attempt to transcribe his unique style
of lecturing, one American journalist went so far as to devise a system
of diacritical marks to represent the elaborate pauses and inflections
that Wilde would use to manipulate his audience. Likewise, Yeats commented famously that Wilde was the only conversationalist he knew
who seemed to speak in perfect sentences. Though Yeats's description
of Wilde is perhaps the best known, Shaw also described his style of
speaking, as did Conan Doyle:

> His conversation left an indelible impression upon my mind. He towered
> above us all, and yet had the art of seeming to be interested in all that we
> could say. He had delicacy of feeling and tact, for the monologue man,
> however clever, can never be a gentleman at heart. He took as well as
> gave, but what he gave was unique. He had a curious precision of state-
> ment, a delicate flavour of humour, and a trick of small gestures to illus-
> trate his meaning, which were peculiar to himself.[34]

Adolphe Retté similarly described Wilde as a "monopolizer of the
conversation"—as someone who had total control and delivered a complete performance.[35] That this artificiality—if one can call it that—is
supposed to signify now as "gay" simply plays into the stereotype that
equates effeminacy with homosexuality, or, at the time, sodomy. Though
this assumption was not the automatic one made about the dandies of
the late eighteenth and early nineteenth centuries, it was one that was
often hinted at and that remained in the background. For Wilde, his

very conversational style was seen to signify his "pathology." Indeed, the enjoyment of his wit—whether at a party or at the theater—was hypocritically reciprocal to the lack of notice given to the practices it was supposed to signify. Wilde pushed against this silence a bit further with almost every major work he produced. As A. J. A. Symons observed:

> Wilde carried the pose much further than any of his forerunners [Brummel, Lytton, D'Orsay], and made explicit what they had implied. Those who knew him well were made to realize that over-careful dress was almost the least of his dandyisms. He appeared to have subdued his existence into a pattern, a formula of elegance lacking at no point in dignity of style. He was never off parade. . . . His most casual utterances were framed in witty flashes, in sentences suited, if not designed, to bear the test of print.[36]

Making explicit what is only suggested by others, Symons attributes much of Wilde's performance to the encoding of his sexual interests: care and precision equal queer. However, even though Symons's appraisal was certainly not a new one, Yeats suggested the same when he commented on Wilde's home life as so filled with "harmony" that it "suggested some deliberate artistic composition.[37] Wilde's precision in his speech and dress, in other words, spilled over into the design—as Symons goes on to note—of every detail of his public life: from what will be served at tea to the wedding bands that he and his wife wore. Rather than becoming more dandified, his persona actually became more securely worldly without crossing the line of public taste—except, perhaps, in the company of Lord Douglas, who often intentionally crossed the performative line. Wilde's performance of self, therefore, should not necessarily be seen as one in which a proto-queer sensibility was being put forth systematically—even though his philosophies of "hedonism" or "aestheticism" suggested as much at one level. Rather, Wilde's performance was an ongoing autobiographical study. As Richard Le Gallienne argues:

> Wilde once said that he gave only his talent to his writings, and kept his genius for his conversation. This was quite true, but it would have been

truer still if he had said that he kept his genius for his life; for his writings . . . are but one illustrative part of him. They contribute to the general effect he strove to produce, the dramatization of his own personality. From the beginning to the end he was a great actor—of himself.[38]

Wilde's performance was part of his self-promotion, which fed his professionalism, but his conversation as performance was also a type of self-writing in which he constantly invented and reinvented himself for a new season, a new group of acquaintances, or the purposes of a new project.[39]

The basis of Wilde's conversation was the elaboration of a metaphor or analogy that he would use to make a point, but which was probably just as likely meant to entertain and show his abilities as a writer. As Henri de Régnier describes: "The ability to tell stories was so natural to him that Wilde spoke for his own benefit. Of their own account his thoughts would take the form of a story or fable, and he would abandon himself to their inexhaustible inspiration. Wilde would tell stories and he would tell them indefinitely."[40]

Indeed, like the perfect embodiment of the romantic ironist that he was, Wilde was able to combine genres even in his conversation to create a sense that his speech was a sort of spoken arabesque in which stories, anecdotes, philosophy, wit, and repartee were combined as if according to a script that he was following in his head—or, at the least, writing as he went along. One account of Wilde's ability to create in this way is Laurence Housman's *Echo de Paris*, which reproduces a meeting between the author and Wilde in Paris in 1899, the year before his death. Subtitled "A Study from Life," the book claims to be an analysis of Wilde but is actually a playlet, with dialogue markers and interpolations of "stage directions" into the text, that reproduces a complete conversation held between Wilde, Robbie Ross, and Housman.[41]

As one would expect, Wilde's conversation here does take the form of a series of elaborate monologues. Indeed, when there is banter back and forth, it is often between Housman and Ross, with Wilde holding back only to join in from time to time with a story of some type, and once he begins, he holds forth until he reaches a dramatic conclusion. What is striking about Housman's book is the way, a mere twenty-five years after the events that he recounts took place, he treats Wilde as a character in a play. The elision of the living Wilde with a fictitious character called "Wilde," of course, is easily suggested by Wilde's own self-creation and the desire in the twentieth century to see him as a symbolic character.[42]

Housman's creation of a playlike structure for which to discuss Wilde illustrates exactly the kind of influence that Wilde as a figure has had since his postprison writing. Wilde has functioned as the type not only of "the homosexual," or more specifically "the effeminate homosexual male," but also of a performative paradigm that blends self-creation with self-promotion to found an extremely influential twentieth-century strain of cultural production.[43] Though perhaps not solely a queer aesthetic, this model of creative and critical deployment of self has its origins in Wilde's own sexuality and the pressure it placed on the rest of his life and work. As Avrom Fleishman notes, "*De Profundis*, as its title . . . suggests, is an exercise in biblical rewriting and in a typological redaction of personal experience.[44] Wilde's reconfiguration of himself in Christian terms—as one who has gone through the "wandering, conversion, and sacramental redemption" of a figure like Guido in Browning's *The Ring and the Book*—shows that, as Koestenbaum speculates, Wilde's reemergence from prison is as a transformative figure whose goal is to lead the way toward a salvation of sorts through the very suffering of his own body. Wilde's re-creation of himself within a tradition of typology, however, might seem like a movement away from his previous role of romantic ironist. However, I would argue that by "fleshing out his own self image via the biblical texts,[45] Wilde is taking the German romantic ideal to its ultimate conclusion. After all, self-creation often ends with a sort of pagan version of typology—Nietzsche, as Fleishman as well as Nancy and Lacoue-Labarthe argue, is simply the more obvious example of this. The difference lies in what Fleishman calls the "bathetic" aspect of Wilde's *De Profundis*, or what Sedgwick, in *Epistemology of the Closet*, terms the "sentimental" nature of his postprison work. The bathos that enters Wilde's writing might seem the obverse of the ironic mode of the rest of his career, but Wilde's shift toward a Christlike image for himself required that he shed the distancing devices of irony for a different realignment toward the victim—or the objectified—as the ultimate subjectivity. *De Profundis* and *The Ballad of Reading Gaol* are not so much attempts at autobiography as they are attempts to formulate two different ways to use the new identities he had been given—invert and criminal—to subvert the accepted stories as they were written.

Picture Perfect

Wilde's development of an identifiable public personality—whether given to him, as it was by Gilbert and Sullivan and the illustrators of *Punch*, or one of his own design—was possible only as the technical means for the reproduction of his type became available. Wilde's concept of his own creation as a type, in other words, could only have the influence it did through the various forms of rapid reproduction of the time such as photography, journalism, and publishing. At the beginning of his career, Wilde fed the nascent system of publicity of the Victorian period by lecturing extensively at a grueling pace that left him little time for anything else. Indeed, Wilde was amazingly adept at using the system of promotion through technology to imprint versions of his personality—or type—to distribute as many ways as he could. It is perhaps not surprising that Jane Gaines begins *Contested Culture: The Image, the Voice, and the Law* with a discussion of Napoleon Sarony's New York photograph of Wilde, taken in the photographer's studio while Wilde was on tour in North America in 1882. Entitled *Oscar Wilde, No. 18*, the image shows Wilde in a typical costume for the tour: velveteen jacket and knickers and his famous long hair.[46] Questions that arise for Gaines are material ones having to do with the ownership or authorship of the image of Wilde in this photograph—of which 85,000 unauthorized copies were in circulation.[47] While I do not want to retrace the complex legal, aesthetic, and cultural arguments raised by this fact, I do want to speculate that Wilde is in many ways the inevitable figure to be at

Oscar Wilde, photographed by Sarony.

the center of such a controversy.[48] The energy that Wilde put into his own image creation—and the way in which Sarony's photo captures both Wilde's "look" of the time and his ability to perform a version of himself—makes Wilde the perfect example of what will appear, in the twentieth century, as the media-savvy, self-promoting artist.

Gaines expertly identifies the complexity of the issues raised by the photograph—most importantly, perhaps, how it constitutes "high" and "low" art. The photo uses the characteristics of the seated portrait but mixes these with the conventions of popular theater. In blending high and low forms, Sarony prefigures questions about what is and is not "original" that will evolve in the twentieth century with particular urgency. By the time of Warhol, the use of high-art signifiers (the portraits of the jet-set rich that Warhol made in the 1980s, for instance) would continue to be reproduced in relation to low-art forms—the aesthetics of the silk screen process—but in a postmodern system of hollow signification. However, "Where does the original reside?" is still an important question. Is originality a part of the author's high-art credentials, or does it lie in the ability of the author to be himself a "star"? Likewise, what is the relationship of either to the mode of reproduction and distribution? Warhol's obsessive control over all aspects of his own artistic production showed his desire to be both author and celebrity, creator and subject. Though Sarony is the "author" of the photograph, Wilde is perhaps no less the author, too, in his ability always to author his own image of himself.

The combination of commissioned portrait and silk screen that provides a tension in Warhol and in the reproduction of Wilde is specifically posited by Gaines in Sarony's photo as "a combination of the aesthetics of the portrait tradition and the wild popularity of the mass-produced *carte de visite*."[49] Indeed, with its relationship to the theater, the *carte de visite* was a part of the star system that Wilde knew only too well as a playwright-to-be and avid fan himself.[50] Almost as if in expectation of the Hollywood star system, he already acted like a celebrity who quite literally—most especially on his American tour—put his talents into his work, but his genius into himself. Wilde solidified a connection, in fact, between the intellectual and the star system by reprocessing the essence of his thought in epigrams that could, like the photos, be reproduced and disseminated via the press, his lectures, and word of mouth.

Gaines suggests that "the showdown between the original and the copy has been staved off, first and most successfully by the Romantic movement, which attempted to ameliorate the deleterious effects of the industrial revolution."[51] Seeing Wilde as an heir of German romanticism is not a contradiction in this case simply because Wilde saw the romantic myth of the author as just that: a historical idea that had rhetorical value but was already doomed by the advent of the modern world—most especially by technology. Wilde's arguments against the ugliness of his contemporary world were more than simply mitigated by his wholehearted participation in that which it offered in the form of pleasures—including the chance to be not only an artist but also a star as perhaps no writer had ever been before. In this sense, Gaines's claim is quite important, that the technological aspects that allowed for a "studio stardom"—as opposed to one based on the theater—were only possible in the United States, and only around the time of Wilde's tour there.[52] It may even be possible to argue that his experiences in the New World provided him with the knowledge he needed to continue to fashion himself along the lines argued by Richard Dyer in his numerous discussions of the Hollywood version of the star.[53] Wilde's influence on twentieth-century performance, therefore, can be linked to what he learned in the United States about the star system and brought back with him to Europe as the vital importance of being Oscar.

PART II

CHAPTER 4

Talking as Performance

Capote's Corpus: *Answered Prayers* and Unfinished Projects

> Sometimes . . . I think about all the dead people who would have loved 54. It's a shame they're not around—people like Ronald Firbank or Toulouse-Lautrec or Baudelaire or Oscar Wilde or Carl Van Vechten.
>
> —Truman Capote

> "Of course, the truth of it is," said Capote, replacing his glasses and sitting up straight, "that the thing I like to do most in the whole world is *talk*."
>
> —Gloria Steinem

Wilde's ability to promote himself—his seemingly innate understanding of publicity—allowed him to use the production of his own image as the lens through which all his other critical, creative, and promotional work could be magnified synergistically. Though Wilde criticized the popular press for "the tyranny that it proposes to exercise over people's private lives," which is "quite extraordinary," he contrasts the situation in England with "America," where "journalism has carried its authority to the grossest and most brutal extreme. As a natural consequence it has begun to create a spirit of revolt. People are amused by it, or disgusted by it. . . . But it is no longer the real force it was. It is not seriously treated."[1] Wilde finds the inability of journalism to shape opinion—or to be taken seriously as an intellectual force—an advantage for the American artist. It is almost as though Wilde foresaw the type of journalism that was to arise in the United States in the latter half of the twentieth century when a figure like Truman Capote would systematically attempt to transform journalism itself into an art form.[2]

In his preface to *The Dogs Bark* (1973), a collection of his journalistic pieces from roughly the time of *In Cold Blood* (1965), Capote focuses on his controversial interview with Marlon Brando entitled "The Duke in His Domain" (1958). Capote's interview was infamous not only for the apparently accurate portrait it painted of Brando as a self-centered and not particularly bright actor but also for the revelations that Capote was able to obtain. Here, however, Capote describes the "Brando profile" as of interest to him for "literary reasons."[3] That is: "What is the lowest level of journalistic art, the one most difficult to turn from a sow's ear into a silk purse? The movie star 'interview' . . . surely nothing could be less easily elevated than that!"[4] Capote was attempting, in other words, to take the very journalism that Wilde described and turn it into a form of art by applying literary craftsmanship to a subgenre that had previously been considered to be out of the realm of serious artistic scrutiny. Like Wilde, however, Capote's division between "art" and supposedly inartistic popular forms such as journalism was somewhat disingenuous in that they both created a name for themselves in the popular press as much as celebrities as artists.[5] Indeed, though Capote did not attempt to master the same number of literary genres that Wilde did, he did feel that there were no real limits to what he might be able to do with the novel form—as can be seen in his plans for his unfinished magnum opus, *Answered Prayers*.

One of the most talented writers of his generation, Capote nevertheless remains a marginal figure in the canon of postwar American literature. He became most widely known for his extension of realist techniques into a recounting of the events and consequences of a multiple murder in Kansas in the first "nonfiction novel," *In Cold Blood* (1966).

But perhaps Capote's most interesting and important artistic development would have been the novel he never finished but apparently worked on from 1966 until his death in 1984. A novel about a bisexual hustler / writer who becomes involved with a mysterious beauty, Kate McCloud, and a plot to kidnap her child, it is filled with the supposedly privileged gossip of the ultrarich as told to Capote in confidence. Capote conceived this book as a fictionalized "variation on the nonfiction novel," or more specifically as a Proustian roman à clef. The consequences of this seemingly contradictory project are significant. With *In Cold Blood*, Capote had tried to bring realism to a new level by making it factual: the nonfiction was a bold attempt at a "real" realism. In effect, *Answered Prayers* was to reflect a literary realism that made privileged claims for fictive realism over the "real" in a world where what was defined as "real," social experience, existed as fiction. As a social novel, *Answered Prayers* was to be based on a literary realism that saw its role as stripping the fictiveness from the social to expose the immateriality of reified social experience in the postmodern era. Capote's project came to an end after the initial publication of four chapters brought a brutal response from the people whose secrets he had listened to for years and now told about in print. No one was more surprised by this outcome than Capote himself.

Indeed, Capote might have held the same position as an artist during his own fin de siècle as Wilde had held for his had Capote been able to finish his aborted project. Already in his early books and in his performance of the role of serious "writer," Capote paralleled Wilde in his use of self-promotion and the ability to sell himself. Even in recent biographies of Wilde and Capote—by Richard Ellmann and Gerald Clarke, respectively—the two figures are linked by the fact that their life stories are told with the same tragic arc, in which they rise to the pinnacle of a type of literary and popular stardom only to fall because of personal weaknesses: homosexual proclivities for Wilde, alcoholism and drug abuse for Capote.

Though British and Commonwealth writers who came to maturity in the beginning of the twentieth century may have had a more material link to Wilde than did Capote, almost all the members of this generation were mowed down—quite literally—in the Great War.[6] Wilde's resuscitation would have to await another generation, until the writers of the thirties—Isherwood, Auden, and the rest—who would live into the post–World War II era. Indeed, Capote made it clear that it is this lineage on which he based his own career by making a much-publicized pilgrimage to Wilde's grave in the 1970s. As late as the year of his death, Capote said that his fascination with Gide—about whom he had written a profile—had much to do with the fact that he had actually known Wilde: "And that always rather impressed me. I had one other friend who had known Oscar Wilde. Oscar Wilde is one of the people that I would have most liked to know. I'm sure that I would have liked him a lot."[7]

Capote built on Wilde not only by mimicking his conversational abilities but also by placing at the center of his writing a form of self-performance that, like Wilde's, was designed to advance his career. His famous Black and White Ball in 1966, nominally a birthday party for his friend Katherine Graham, was also a publicity stunt calculated to take full advantage of the celebrity he had gained by the publication of *In Cold Blood*.[8] Indeed, Capote often bragged about his ability at self-promotion and the fact that he had never needed to hire an agent. When *In Cold Blood* was published, his face appeared on the covers of the *New York Times Book Review* and *Newsweek* simultaneously—a feat orchestrated solely by him. In fact, Capote's ability to create himself as news was heralded early in his career when he supposedly published at age ten his first piece of writing, "Mrs. Busybody," in the *Mobile Register*. Based on an actual person in the town of Monroeville, Capote's hometown in Alabama, the piece created a scandal when the newspaper refused to print the second installment after discovering that the story was based on a real person. Likewise, Capote's first published book, *Other Voices, Other Rooms* (1948)—a southern gothic coming-out story—was almost overshadowed by the photograph of the author on the back cover: an extremely young-looking man draped on a chaise longue faces the camera with a decidedly queer, cold stare. Looking like a devilish child, Capote was unabashedly "out" from the beginning of his career. Like Warhol after him, he never pretended to be anything other than what he was. Like Byron's and Wilde's before him, Capote's effeminacy was calculated to indicate homosexuality, though in a much more direct and unmitigated way.

If Capote's queer heritage was not in question, neither was his ability to promote himself as a conversationalist. Capote argued several times in print that great conversationalists are in fact really monologists, and he illustrated this principle often via the televised talk show. In 1959, for example, he appeared with Norman Mailer and Dorothy Parker on David Susskind's *Open End*. When the conversation turned to a discussion of the literary merits of Jack Kerouac, Mailer attempted to defend him, while Capote announced that Kerouac's work "isn't writing at all—it's merely typing."[9] The next day, as Mailer himself has written, what was remembered from the show was Capote's bon mot; Mailer—the better-known writer—might as well have been absent.[10] Capote's subsequent rise to fame rested in large part on his ability to render a description of someone or something—often spoken in a wonderfully bitchy voice—in a memorably concise image. Like Wilde, Capote used this performative ability to open doors for himself both professionally and socially. He was, by the 1970s and 1980s, a celebrity known to many people precisely because of his appearances on *The Tonight Show* or *Merv Griffin*, where his personality itself—or his ability to perform a self—was the main attraction. It is not surprising that his last major journalistic project, his collection entitled *Music for Chameleons* (1980), was written for Warhol's *Interview* magazine, as the emphasis on talk—on pure personality, such as one would find in the celebrity interviews that made up this publication—could be seen as a version of the pure expression of personality theorized by Schlegel and Wilde.[11]

In the preface to *Music for Chameleons*, Capote acknowledges the firestorm created by his publication in *Esquire* of the chapters of *Answered Prayers* but refutes the idea that he stopped writing and publishing his opus for that reason. Rather, he claims that he discovered "an apparently unsolvable problem, and if I couldn't solve it, I might as well quit writing. The problem was: how can a writer successfully combine within a single form—say the short story—all he knows about every other form of writing?"[12] Capote felt that his writing style was becoming successively more encrusted and that the completed chapters of *Answered Prayers* were "insufficiently illuminated."[13] *Music for Chameleons*, therefore, was supposed to represent his going "back to kindergarten" to relearn his art so that he could write in such a way that he would not be "restricting myself to the techniques of whatever form I was working in" but rather "using everything I knew about writing—all I'd learned from film scripts, plays, reportage, poetry, the short story, novellas, the novel."[14] Though it was perhaps difficult not to see Capote's new book as a diversion from the reaction to *Answered Prayers*, *Music for Chameleons* offers as the answer to the crisis of *Answered Prayers* a new form of writing that Capote would call the "conversational portrait."

This new form shared much with both the reinvention of the dialogue form of Schlegel and Wilde and Warhol's experiments with redacted monologues and conversations in his *A: A Novel* (1968) and, later, in *Interview*. Capote's version, however, allowed him not only to work with dialogue but to insert himself directly into the story he was telling, thus blurring the line separating not only fact from fiction but also life from art. Though the longest piece written in this mode, "Handcarved Coffins," is similar in both subject matter and quality to the best writing in *In Cold Blood*, the new collection was less impressive as writing qua writing than the extant chapters of *Answered Prayers*. Yet in this new work, Capote seemed less invested in what he wrote than in the idea that this new form allowed him to bring his entire arsenal of technical knowledge to each new piece. How exactly this form allowed him to do this—and, especially, how it was to be applied to *Answered Prayers*—was never clear.

Capote's new manner of writing was in essence a stripping away of everything but dialogue and a minimum amount of description. Any interpellation within the dialogue is set off in parentheses, as if to suggest that this material was placed in the text at a later date in an attempt to clarify what was happening. At the beginning of each piece, the exposition is rendered concisely as in a play: "Time: November, 1970. Place: Los Angeles International Airport. I am sitting inside a telephone booth. It is a little after eleven in the morning."[15] Indeed, Capote compares his technique to that of a movie. Praising what he sees as the ability of Lillian Ross's published account of the making of the film version of *The Red Badge of Courage*, Capote wished to be able to reproduce her method: "its fast cuts, its flash forward and back, it was itself like a movie, and as I read it I wondered what would happen if the author let go of her hard linear straight-reporting discipline and handled her material as if it were fictional . . . ?"[16] In an attempt to provide an answer to this question, he went on to write *The Muses Are Heard* (1956), his first fictionlike reportage. From the beginning, Capote suggests, it was the ability to write in a way that allowed him to combine all the genres that most interested him about the nonfiction novel form itself. His new work in *Music for Chameleons*, therefore, was an attempt—at least in his own mind—to carry this goal further by refining the technique, if not the aim, of this type of writing. Capote hoped, in other words, to create a new way to write cinematically—to find a way to combine genres and effects.

Indeed, Capote's last two books attempted not only to strip away the lines that separate types of writing but also to erode further the difference between art and autobiography. In constructing *Answered Prayers* as a roman à clef, he claimed to want to do the opposite of what this form usually accomplished. In 1980 he argued that by writing *Answered Prayers*, "my intentions are . . . to remove disguises, not manufacture them." In writing *Music for Chameleons*, he went further by insisting that everything he wrote was true. With both books Capote was much bolder about representing previously taboo subject matter—from gay hustling to gruesome stories with implications about people in high places. His new tendency to tell it "like it is" was made especially apparent in the fact that he himself appears as a character in every story. Though these appearances tend to lend the pieces an air of immediacy, he resists the temptation to make each story be about himself. Indeed, only in the self-interview at the end of the book—"Nocturnal

Turnings, or How Siamese Twins Have Sex," seemingly a companion piece to "Self-Portrait (1972)"—does Capote really place himself front and center.

Like Wilde's self-examination for mass consumption, *De Profundis*, Capote's "Nocturnal Turnings" can be seen as a self-portrait during times of crisis. Just as Wilde uses self-analysis as therapy in *De Profundis*, so Capote proclaims famously: "But I'm not a saint yet. I'm an alcoholic. I'm a drug addict. I'm homosexual. I'm a genius."[17] What Capote seems to suggest here is that the form of the book itself is the self as theater.[18] That is, though he is scrupulous about downplaying his own personality in the pieces in the book, he is also aware that writing about other people involves creating a holographic picture of himself—with each character presented as part of a composition made real by one's ability to play them, from one's own mind, correctly. Though Capote prides himself on his ability to frame the other person—hence the title to the last section is also called "Conversational Portraits"—he is also aware that what he is involved in is an experimentation with style.

In fact, Capote signals this experimentation with references to not only painting but also music by using the book's title as the title to the first section. The attempt to use art forms other than writing to represent the effects that he is trying to achieve is worthy of Wilde following Schlegel and suggests what Capote implicitly wanted: a form to combine not only all genres of writing but also the effects of different media as well.[19] Though the book's title, *Music for Chameleons*, also suggests, perhaps unfortunately, that Capote saw his work as a series of finger exercises, a rehearsal before approaching once again the symphony that was to be the revamped *Answered Prayers*, at another level Capote was suggesting that the plurality of the book's interests—the modulated phasing between description and dialogue, autobiography and doctored fact, stardom and the quotidian—was a new way to make music: a new form invented for those who understood, like the chameleon, that changing one's color often is a way to survive.

Capote's emphasis on the spoken word—his ability to shape fiction out of his conversations with various people he knew—places him within a tradition of queer self-performance that was enormously important for Anglo-American literary culture of both the nineteenth and twentieth centuries. Capote's movement toward a pure form of conversation as art not only makes literal what Wilde's *Earnest* implies but can also be seen as an inevitable telos for many gay and lesbian writers of the twentieth century. The novels of Isherwood, for example, move from the somewhat closeted early novels of his British phase (*All the Conspirators* [1928]), to the more explicitly queer work of his Berlin period (*Mr. Norris Changes Trains* [1935]), to the fictionalized autobiography of his California writing (*A Single Man* [1964]), which ends in his published diaries (*October* [1982]). Similarly, Capote stripped away the baroque trappings of his earlier writing—especially his southern gothic stories and novellas—to make more explicit their autobiographical nature. This movement toward underwriting may also have been a movement toward some type of postcontemporary form for queer writing—one that was not only a further experimentation with nonfictional forms and self-writing but also a search for a way to express the queer sensibility at work in one's performance of self.

Toward this end, Capote's work needs to be reconsidered for its construction of a gay aesthetic or cultural practice in the vital period stretching from World War II through the 1970s. From *Other Voices, Other Rooms*, which modifies the literary traditions of southern realism and gothicism to present what is essentially a vision of gay identity in the South, to *Answered Prayers*, which takes up the idea of the gay (or bisexual) male perspective as a privileged view of social experience, Capote's writings and his career are an important gauge of gay cultural practice in contemporary American life. Indeed, the canon of gay male fiction in the twentieth century is a compendium of themes and tropes promulgated by Wilde in his writing.

The first chapter of *Answered Prayers*, "Unspoiled Monsters," is one long dissertation on the gay literary world of the twentieth century as recounted through a story told by the protagonist, P. B. Jones, of his relationship with "Denny Fouts," the same character who shows up in Isherwood's *Down There on a Visit* (1962) as the world's most famous prostitute.[20] In telling the story of Fouts, Capote's narrator mentions in passing not only Isherwood but Stein, Collette, Cocteau, and Rorem, among others. Indeed, Fouts is the perfect figure for tying together a disparate mix of real-life and semifictitious characters who form a sort of who's who of the gay/lesbian *bohème* of the pre– and post–World War II eras. Capote, in other words, has found a way to connect the upper crust of society—as symbolized by the "swans" who appear in "La Cote Basque, 1965"—to the gay underworld of the earlier part of the century to create a continuum stretching from Wilde to the present time of the novel's action.[21] The mood of nineteenth-century Europe is invoked by Capote as part of the backdrop for the novel as he makes causal connections between the private lives of individuals and the public events that shape a national event. The chapter ends with an infamous and thinly veiled encounter between Jones and "Mr. Wallace," aka Tennessee Williams, who purchases his services. Though Capote actually shows an acute sense of Williams's personal problems, he also paints such a candid portrait of the writer that it caused one of the many *Esquire* scandals.[22] The attempt to map out this literary culture was, however, a brave and complicated one. Indeed, by writing a book in the early seventies that could not help but offend just about everyone, Capote was making literal many of the clichés about gay culture in general and himself in particular: that gossip could, in the proper hands, be an art form.[23] He now planned to do on a grand scale what he claimed to have done with his interview of Brando: to update Proust by crafting a structure in which to retell society stories that would also be a work of fiction.

The mixing of gay and straight in a milieu of social decadence powered by the money of the rich provides the novel with an atmosphere much like a gossipy luncheon come to life—perhaps a fantasy for Proust as imagined by Capote. When Jones meets with the friend who first arranges for him to become a prostitute, Jones discusses his theory of writing:

> Because something is true doesn't mean that it's convincing, either in life or in art. Think of Proust. Would *Remembrance* have the ring that it does

if he had made it historically literal, if he hadn't transposed sexes, altered events and identities? If he had been absolutely factual, it would have been less believable, but . . . it might have been better. Less acceptable, but better.[24]

Jones's disquisition on Proust is, of course, a comment on the book one is reading. He finishes the speech by declaring, "I don't care what anybody says about me as long as it isn't true." He then describes his own novel, which will be "a report. An account. Yes, I'll *call* it a novel."[25] The working title is *Answered Prayers*. The first chapter of the actual *Answered Prayers*, in other words, lays out the plan for the whole book: the Proustian plot, the desire to do a roman à clef, the mixing of actual gossip with made-up (or sometimes purposely mixed up) invention, and the attempt to re-create the real world to make it better than it actually is. In other words, Capote attempted to fashion his own queer world— like the real one, only better.

Matching his desire to experiment with storytelling and the novel form was Capote's equally audacious attempt to stretch the limits of what was considered acceptable subject matter. Though Capote began thinking about *Answered Prayers* at least as early as the 1950s, the advent of the 1970s allowed him freedom not only to name names but also to represent aspects of a gay subculture in New York that would have been unthinkable for a major writer before that time. Indeed, "Mojave," originally the second chapter, sparked accusations of misogyny because of attitudes toward women expressed by one of its characters that caused a scandal at the time of its magazine publication. Similarly the title of the planned last chapter, "Father Flanagan's All-Night Nigger-Queen Kosher Cafe"—a reference to a place mentioned in the first chapter, "Unspoiled Monsters"—is seemingly an attempt on Capote's part to insult nearly everyone. Described by Fouts while he is in a drug-induced high as "rock bottom,"[26] the place "where they throw you off at the end of the line,"[27] it is also an imaginary realm that he longs to get to with the help of drugs, a home for "outcast[s] . . . yids, nigs, spiks, fags, dykes, dope fiends, and commies."[28] While Capote spares no one the ignominy of name-calling and stereotypical labels, his inclusion of such objectionable material may have been something more than merely an early reaction to "political correctness," as it is likely that Capote wanted his novel to be about crossing boundaries.[29] Not only does Jones move between gay and straight, upper crust and the street, he embodies the seventies notion of the swinger, of someone who lives two or more lives—a character that we will see at the end of the decade in films such as *Looking for Mr. Goodbar* (1977) and *American Gigolo* (1980). Jones is the model of the artist because he can do what Capote could: move from circle to circle, be at home anywhere. Capote suspended outward signs of judgment so that everyone would accept him. He saw his own ability to have friends and acquaintances of all sexes, races, classes, and sexualities as a strength and as one of the factors that allowed for the very existence of *Answered Prayers*.

That Capote was also creating a figure who could embody the seventies notion of transgression—and it limits—may well have been a historical convergence, as it is difficult to imagine Capote publishing these chapters during any other decade. In fact, Capote's representation of sexuality may well have been an acknowledgment that the roles that keep identities apart—and hence intact—were failing. It is not surprising that the next step beyond *In Cold Blood* would be to create a work of pure gossip, of the unadulterated telling of real stories in a fictional form that showed that the stable worlds of literary and cultural distinction were eroding—or would be seen to from the vantage point of what we might now call a queer sensibility. *Answered Prayers* was Capote's attempt to queer the nonfictional novel in order to break not only new formal and generic paradigms but social and ethical ones as well. That Capote did this while attempting to fashion a huge edifice in which to hold his effects in place was a stupendous goal—perhaps one that could never be attained. If he had succeeded, he might have pointed the way toward a new direction for American fiction. As it is, he may well have inspired, if not foreseen, a development that took fiction beyond the blurring of itself with fact and toward the construction of entire novels around the underside of cultural erosion in which the members of a social set are emblematic of a country's political and ethical health. With the advent of the "brat pack" novels of the Reagan years, for example, Capote may well have spawned a proto–Gen X version of his own unfinished work.[30]

As an attempt to answer a crisis in *Answered Prayers*, it will never be clear whether or not *Music for Chameleons* solved any problems for Capote. The short story "Mojave," the original second chapter of *Answered Prayers* before Capote decided to exclude it, was not rewritten for its inclusion in *Music for Chameleons*, nor was the new form in which most of *Music for Chameleons* is written—the conversational portrait—a viable one in which to rewrite it. Capote, who had never had an outright failure, seemed hesitant to complete his grand project, and after the publication of *Music for Chameleons*, it probably became an impossibility—at least in the version that he had described for so many years. Though at least two other chapters were written, and were read by Capote's editor, they have never been found. The one new work that did appear, the short story "One Christmas," is reminiscent of Capote's best stories, though the flat, lackluster style in which it is written—possibly the new "underwriting" that he was planning *Music* to inaugurate—did not bode well for a resurgence for Capote and may, as many critics suggested, simply have been the result of a deteriorating mental state he was no longer able to arrest.

In a foreword to Lawrence Grobel's *Conversations with Capote*, James A. Michener likens Capote to both Cocteau and Wilde as "artists" who "are sometimes outrageously against the grain" and thus "help keep society . . . more civilized than it would otherwise be."[31] Michener's compliment is backhanded and homophobic, but he is accurate in noting that Capote was at least playing the role of the great artist in respect to contemporary society.[32] Indeed, Capote's most frequent response to questions about how he felt about the reaction that greeted *Answered Prayers* was to exclaim, "But I'm an artist! What did they expect?" Echoing the plaint of the decadent, Capote retreated into the role of the self-conscious artiste more and more—perhaps as a response to his being snubbed by high society after the appearance of *Answered Prayers*. His high-art pretensions—which reminded Brendan Gill of Wilde as early as the 1940s, when Capote worked for the *New Yorker* as an office boy—

were in concert with Michener's beliefs that because *Answered Prayers* is "a *roman à clef* summarizing a period," Capote "has a better chance of being the central figure of our period than any of the rest of us may have."[33]

In 1982, two years before he died, Capote told Grobel that he was wrong to say in *Music for Chameleons* that he needed a new form of writing to use all "of the powers at [his] command."[34] Though Capote still maintained "that all literature is ultimately gossip,"[35] he felt that he had always been working at full force throughout his career, and that he was, in fact, still planning to publish *Answered Prayers*. By the next year— apparently, the summer of 1983—his longtime friend John Knowles would have a conversation with him in which Capote reportedly said, "I've used up a lot. A lot. And . . . now . . . when I look at what I'm currently working on . . . I find out that . . . it isn't really . . . very good."[36] Knowles is convinced, in fact, that Capote destroyed a large manuscript at this time that he had once shown him and that contained all that he had written of *Answered Prayers*—perhaps the entire book—which Knowles failed to read when he had the chance. Capote died the following summer.

Capote's influence on queer performance can be seen not merely in his desire to fashion a sensational persona with which to promote his publications but also in his attempts to redefine the concept of stardom for an author of his generation. Understanding his canniness at doing this is part of understanding Capote as a performer. His ability always to speak well and entertainingly was a by-product, at least in part, of his Alabama upbringing—a milieu on rich display in John Berendt's *Midnight in the Garden of Good and Evil* (1994), a book that is itself an extension of Capote's work in local color reportage. While Capote was able to play himself convincingly on the lecture circuit or on talk shows, his one attempt at translating his persona into a traditional performance was an overwhelming failure. In the film *Murder by Death* (1976),[37] Capote stars as the eccentric millionaire Lionel Twain, who has invited the world's greatest detectives to his manor house to solve a murder that is to be committed in their presence. Though the film's hackneyed plot is supposed to mirror those of popular detective writers, Capote's role, as written by Neil Simon, was actually based on Capote himself and would seem to have been a safe bet. Yet for someone normally so astute at playing himself, Capote's self-performance here is hopelessly flat and awkward. After filming was over, he said that he had hoped that making the movie would be "a lark," but it turned out to be "a bore."[38] Simon and the director were, in fact, playing off Capote's own spoof of himself as a supposedly evil character as seen on the cover of *Esquire*'s publication of "Unspoiled Monsters," where Capote is shown dressed in black while fingering a stiletto. In part a reference to his penchant for large hats (to cover his experiments with hair transplants), Capote's gangsterish image became the look that people associated with him for the rest of his life. He became, in other words, a sort of queer Dashiell Hammett—an Al Capone of the literary world. This image, created in large part with the help of the media, permeates the film's several jokes made in reference to his homosexuality and culminates in the fact that the solution to the movie's puzzle is that the maid (played by Nancy Walker) is in fact Capote in disguise.

Indeed, Capote's floppy gray fedora ("Forgive the theatrics. I love illusions" are his first lines) is used as the mark of gender undecidability. Worn by both the maid and the butler, who at one point does a mincing walk (as played by Alec Guinness), the hat becomes symbolic of a

Truman Capote in *Murder by Death*.

running joke throughout the film: that the mystery world's most macho dick, Sam Diamond (Spade), played by Peter Falk, and most effeminate (as played by David Niven) are both in the closet. "Twain" therefore reflects this dual nature and provides the viewer with the best clue to the film's mystery. In terms of popular culture, the movie's use of Capote as a 1970s pop icon is filtered through his ability to perform himself (or, in this case, really to fail to) and the ways in which this performance was automatically marked as gay and ambiguous. By the mid-1970s, Capote's identity as a queer literary phenomenon had become so widely known that audiences for a movie as popular as this one were expected to understand his "character" as a self-satire that fit into the other performances in the movie: Falk had played Colombo, Elsa Lanchester a maid in *Witness for the Prosecution* (1957), and so forth. Capote's character, in other words, references both his *Answered Prayers* persona as the bad boy of publishing who symbolically stabs his friends in the back as well as his literary/performative notoriety as an out gay man. Like Wilde, Capote had become a character in a work based loosely on his own life.[39] Their lives, constructed as fiction, make for irresistible retellings. The authors seem to realize that what a reader wants in these works is a way for both men—even only for the duration of a couple of hours—to be brought back to life. One wishes to hear them speak.

Warhol's Factory Seconds

Can't I deduct liquor if I have to get high to talk and talking's my business?

—Andy Warhol

The opposite of talking isn't listening. The opposite of talking is waiting.

—Fran Lebowitz

The one artist who took Capote's involvement with Wildean performance to a new level—beyond the self as star and into the concept of the self as media empire—was his onetime spookily devoted fan Andy Warhol. In a conversation between Capote and Warhol recorded in 1973, the latter told the former that "the way you can describe things, they're so many exciting things you could use someday in stories and things like that. Just the stories you're saying now, they're really unusual, and they sound so, you know, interesting. I mean, even just visually—."[40] Capote responds to this suggestion by remarking, "But things have to fit in. Everything, after all, is a work of art, not feathers of a fan." Warhol had indeed hit on the very technique that Capote was to develop seven years later in Warhol's magazine—the conversations that were ultimately collected as *Music for Chameleons*. Warhol was also describing what he probably liked best about Capote's writing: what he calls its unusualness was the writing's reflection of Capote himself.

Warhol moved to New York from Pittsburgh to work as an illustrator of women's shoes, and Capote was perhaps his first obsession with a "star." Warhol wanted to meet Capote in order to illustrate his short stories; however, the lengths to which he went to get to know Capote were extreme. Warhol described these events in *Popism* (1980), his history of the 1950s and 1960s:

> In the fifties, in my pre-Pop days, I wanted to illustrate his [Capote's] short stories so badly I used to pester him with phone calls all the time till one day his mother told me to cut it out. It's hard to say now what it was that made me want to connect my drawings with those short stories. Of course, they were wonderful, very unusual—Truman was a pretty unusual character himself—they were all about sensitive boys and girls in the South who were a little bit outside society and made up fantasies for themselves. I could almost picture Truman tilting his head and arranging his words around the pages, making them go together in a magical way that put you in a certain mood when you read them.[41]

This version of the story, similar to the one that Warhol also records in *The Philosophy of Andy Warhol* (1975), points to his fascination with Capote's ability not only to create himself in his fiction but also to put the reader into a certain "mood" that "in a magical way" created the "unusual character" of Capote himself. Warhol was, in other words, interested—even obsessed—with Capote as a character, or rather with the image of Capote that came through in his writings, which Warhol would fantasize as being the writer. In other words, Warhol was at least as fascinated by what he imagined the writer of the stories would be like as he was with the writings themselves. Capote was, for Warhol, a nexus of desires that for a queer child growing up in an immigrant community in Pittsburgh provided an escape through identification.

Suffering from the ostracism of the macho action painters who then dominated the New York art scene,[42] Warhol found in Capote, before the advent of pop art culture, the illustration of many of his own interests in queer characters and conversation that were present in Capote's writing and later central to Warhol's own achievements. It is difficult to underestimate just how out of the closet Capote's early southern-themed writing was, not to mention his own behavior, manner of speaking, and public persona. Not unlike Frank O'Hara and John Ashbery, Warhol and Capote were to create queer work that provided an alternative to mainstream straight culture.[43] With the advent of pop art, gay artists such as Jasper Johns and Robert Rauschenberg usurped the virility of the action and nonobjectivist schools in New York, though they failed to render in their work clues as to what their preferences were. Warhol, like O'Hara, was much more explicit. His early pop successes, such as *Fifteen Drawings Based on the Writings of Truman Capote* (1952) or the decorated penises in *Boy Book* (1956), were much more explicitly queer than anything being done by anyone else at that time.

Not only did Warhol share Capote's interests, but he was, of course, to become as well known, if not better known, than Capote himself. Though they were written about in the gossip columns as regulars and friends at Studio 54 in the late 1970s, Bob Colacello, the actual editor of *Interview* during this time, argues that Warhol eventually tired of Capote and essentially turned the relationship between Capote and the magazine over to him. However, it was Warhol who had the original idea of taping Capote once a month and publishing the results in

Interview—essentially, following him around with a tape recorder and then having Brigid Polk transcribe and edit the conversation. The technical unfeasibility of doing this, however, was soon apparent, and the only solution was to allow Capote to write his own column instead. "Conversations with Capote" eventually became *Music for Chameleons*. The conversations were actual ones remembered, written down, and then shaped by Capote into what was to become his new form of writing. Warhol's desire to transcribe actual conversation as literature was one that he shared with Capote, though for Warhol the shaping aspect was not what was important—the mere recording of it was.[44] For Warhol, in other words, the selecting of the subject and the lightest editing were the only choices that needed to be made. His goals were in some ways similar to Capote's, yet his method was quite different.

In fact, Warhol's approach to filmmaking was not dissimilar. He avoided technological sophistication in his cinema—even zoom shots or pans—in favor of editing his films whenever he could simply by starting and stopping the camera. His favorite directorial "technique" was to record scenes with a completely stationary camera, which allowed characters to walk in and out of the scene at will.[45] Warhol preferred the equivalent method in his audio experiments. In his novel *A*, he records several days of conversation with his gay "superstar" Ondine, who was famous for his appearance as "the Pope" in *Chelsea Girls* (1966). Warhol's conversations with Ondine merely frame his clever stream-of-consciousness monologues. However, the chapter titles, though from Ondine's words, bespeak the sensibility of Warhol: "dick was bent the right way," "a favor that they blow you," "on the rim," and especially "to B." Similarly, Warhol's *Index* (1967) is a compendium of graphics and interviews in which he speaks at times as someone else. In one instance, he claims to be the son of a refrigerator repairman from Dothan, Alabama. Warhol proceeds to tell very convincing stories of his hometown, probably told to him by his boyfriend of the time, Rod La Rod, who really was from Alabama. Here and in *Interview*, Warhol created a style of writing that was actually the compilation of the words of others. Even his books from the 1970s were, in large part, written by

Polk and Pat Hackett. Only his diaries—taped telephone conversations that he had with Hackett to catalog his expenses for the IRS—can be considered anything like the recording of his actual speech or thoughts.

In his posthumous diaries, Warhol was ultimately to apply the same techniques to himself that he had to Ondine and others. Like Capote and Wilde, Warhol's ultimate queer form of art was a fusion of conversation and autobiography. Like Schlegel, he saw it as a way to combine heterogeneous materials—the randomness of daily events that he recorded in part because he was an avid and catholic collector—in a form that would not only contain everything but present it all as art. If Schlegel dreamed of a type of writing that would be the perfect pluralistic form for the post-Enlightenment artistic enterprise, Warhol saw his own "writing" as pop art's answer to what one does when one is not painting: a project ancillary to his others, but symbolically important and increasingly central to the Factory as his literary/audio experiments were carried out in the form of the Colacello-edited *Interview*.

In the conversation from 1973, Capote says that the kind of writing he was interested in could be described as "sociological."[46] In fact, Capote's most difficult task with *In Cold Blood* was to keep himself out of the story, as he wanted his method to represent a form of purely objective recording that was not unlike Warhol's. As can be seen in *Music for Chameleons*, Capote was to go on to find a way to interject himself into his work. Warhol, who sincerely believed that "frigid people can really make it,"[47] was extremely serious about removing himself from his work at all times. On this point, Capote and Warhol diverge, though it is clear that their two approaches are actually remarkably similar at times and, in fact, herald the approach of stardom as news. Indeed, they were both working in an early version of this milieu with their involvement with *Interview* during the early 1980s. Colacello published his adventures at jet-set parties in his column "out," and Fran Lebowitz published chapters of her aestheticist musings on pop society in "I Cover the Waterfront." While Capote's interviews turned people's conversations and lives into art, the magazine's other contributors implicitly questioned where their journalism stopped being stories about themselves to tell to friends and became something else. The lines blurred between self-interview, gossip, chat, and analysis. The idea that life could be summed up in a series of aphorisms, as in Lebowitz's pieces, was carried to a new plateau. Even Warhol, who had always used the most vacuous, yet sly, epigrams imaginable to discuss his work and interests, tried his hand (at least in theory) in his *Philosophy* to create whole chapters that consisted of floating epigrams loosely assembled under topics such as "Beauty" or "Work." Warhol even takes an aphorism of Capote's—"that certain kinds of sex are total, complete manifestations of nostalgia"—and refines the quip in his own way: "Sex is a nostalgia for when you used to want it, sometimes. Sex is nostalgia for sex."[48] Indeed, Warhol's entire book is constructed as an elaborate conversation between "A" and "B"—a frame that feminizes everyone in the book (or makes everyone a gay man) but also sets up an interchangeable system of identity, an erotic economy. Of course, much of what is discussed by "A" is Warhol's own version of fetishistic consumable late capitalist commodity culture with a sexual twist: money, candy, underwear, consuming, deciding, discerning. The objects and desires mentioned recreate or illustrate much of the philosophy itself.

"Andy made being famous more famous," Lebowitz notes.[49] And indeed that is exactly the project of Warhol Enterprises during the eighties. After his near-fatal shooting by Valerie Solanis in 1968, Warhol retreated into the world of the jet set, replacing the Factory regulars of the sixties with rich people, celebrities, and royals. One of the results was the transformation of *Interview* into a magazine almost wholly about fame, with the process of becoming famous chronicled either in the one-page bios of hunky young stars that always began each issue or in the main section, which usually included an interview with the cover star based on a "conversation" at lunch with Andy and either another editor or a friend. Each cover, though only rarely by Warhol, expressed the Warhol mystique at that time: a celebrity, almost always instantly recognizable, is painted in a faux-pop style in which the person's face appears as if on a poster, with color inked in such a way as to belie the realism of the image as a portrait and to suggest instead a graphic composition—an advertisement. The iconic treatment of any-one who appeared on the cover also added to the idea that the cover had a "star" each issue. Of course, this treatment was undercut to some extent by the newsprintlike paper the magazine was printed on, which seemed to suggest the fleeting nature of fame. It was often difficult to know in *Interview* when something was an article or an ad. Scant text, combined with often first-rate photography, created an inevitable moment of dislocation whenever one turned the page. Is this a Versace ad or a photo of someone being interviewed? Is this a "model" or a "beautiful person"? Is this art or advertisement? *Interview*, in its very design and implementation, became in some ways the best example of the extension of Warhol's pop ideas to question where glitz and hype became art and culture—as mediated, always, via commerce.

Warhol's design for the Factory included his famous work ethic—obvious in the name itself—which meant that hustling himself and his entourage also meant making money. But Warhol's interest in creating stars was also part of a desire to worship them himself. His often starstruck attitude toward celebrities, though at times belied by his comments about them later, was a part of his pop aesthetic. That is, though he championed the ordinariness of things—soup and fame in the United States—he also worshiped whatever had the allure of glamour. As Andrew Ross notes, Warhol probably "offended some intellectuals" when he discussed art because of his "attention to *economy*" and his suggestion "that art had something more directly to do with products, consumers, markets than it had to do with fighting the 'good fight' or with the aesthete's windless realm of great art."[50] The bottom line was art as commodity—and it was up to him to make it. Only in this way, by embracing the schlock and selling it as high art, could a real profit be turned. His belief in an economy of selling and consuming was his idea of an erotics and an aesthetics, too.[51]

During the times in which Capote's and Warhol's careers were at their respective peaks, each was in his own way a symbol of not only artistic but also financial success. The mode of romantic self-dramatization that both men exploited was a way not only to have both

AUGUST $2.00

Cover of *Interview* magazine.

critical and commercial success but also to capitalize on aspects of their talents that were not strictly related to their creative skills. What was singularly important for each was the ability to create cutting-edge artistic work that was connected to, and popularized by, the mode of self-performance begun by Byron and brought into the twentieth century by Wilde in the form of a queer deconstruction of the economic categories of each era. Certainly Capote and Warhol were only two of the more visible examples of the inheritance of Wilde's sense of literary self-performance. They were also, however, merely the generational heirs and shared with other artists aspects of the Wildean paradigm. Capote's experimentation with diaries and, especially, with the attempt to make of his life's encounters and experiences a new type of writing may have been executed more successfully in Isherwood's novels or in Lillian Hellman's trilogy of memoirs. Hellman's writing—closer to Isherwood's elegantly centered prose than Capote's fast-cutting reportage—suggested a way to shape memoirs into short stories. But Capote was able, like Wilde and Warhol, to recycle himself more than once. Just as Wilde used his own epigrams in different conversational and literary contexts, Warhol brought seriality to new heights (or depths) by signaling that it was all that art was—indeed, that it could ever be. Capote, similarly, recycled stories, with the best ones ending up in his writing. Like oral or cinematic tape loops that play on into oblivion, Capote and Warhol constructed their works not only to mirror themselves but also to act as machines to reproduce their own philosophies and opinions, observations and pronouncements: to be them in their untimely absence from the scene.[52]

Hockney's Bigger Splashes

For the generation of gay artists after Warhol, being out from the beginning of their careers was more widely assumed, perhaps mirroring the more available sources of gay images and references. The painter David Hockney, for example, found his primary influences not only in canonic literature but in soft-core pornographic magazines as well. Hockney assumed that his work would reflect his homosexuality in an extremely autobiographical way. His earliest paintings, completed when he was in art school in England, included titles such as *Queer* (1960), *Third Love Painting* (1960), and *Going to Be a Queen for Tonight* (1960), as well as several paintings that refer to Whitman—such as *Adhesiveness* (1960) and *We Two Boys Together Clinging* (1961). Hockney's subject matter became even more directly autobiographical after his visits and eventual move to Los Angeles in the later 1960s. In the early work painted in Los Angeles, such as *Domestic Scene, Los Angeles* (1963) or *Boy Taking a Shower* (1962), Hockney shows his fascination for the male body as it was now available to him in the gay world of Southern California. Hockney attempted to create his own queer way of picturing what was to him a homoerotic paradise. In later paintings, he used his friends and lovers as models and was unflinching in his representation of queer desire and friendship in its private, as well as in its more public, aspects.

Though his painting was not as influenced by commercial illustration and painting as Warhol's, Hockney's famous early paintings of Los Angeles show his acute awareness of commercial advertising. Like Warhol, Hockney composed his paintings by first taking a photograph of an actual scene or person with a Polaroid camera and then transferring the basic composition to canvas—often using bright primary colors in an attempt to suggest the even light of the Southern California sun. Works such as *Two Boys in a Pool, Hollywood* (1965) and *American Collectors (Fred and Marcia Weisman)* (1968) suggest Warhol's use of color.[53] Like Warhol, Hockney also created an autobiography from journals recorded on audiotapes.[54] Hockney goes even further, however, by constructing his oeuvre in such a way that one can, by connecting the titles and sequences of his works, clearly discern the important figures in his life—even the places he has lived and worked or just visited—from the 1960s until today. Unabashedly forthright about his life, Hockney has made his art—whether painting, photography, or drawing—reflect his life's various chapters.

Hockney's ability to catalog the stages of his personal life is brought out in a "quasi-documentary portrait" of the artist directed by Jack Hazan, entitled *A Bigger Splash* (1974). Hazan uses Hockney's actual friends and lovers as "characters," as well as his paintings of them and the settings where the paintings' compositions first suggested themselves, blurring the line between "being and role-playing." As Jack Babuscio goes on to argue, "This convention appears to suit Hockney, whose deceptive innocence and disorienting self-created face (platinum blonde hair, owl-rimmed spectacles) exhibit a special feeling for performance and a flair for the theatrical." Indeed, Babuscio concludes that though Hazan's portrait of Hockney "remains . . . a subjective record of *one* gay life in which the conjunction of fantasy and experience make common cause, it does effectively isolate the strong strain of protest that resides in the gay sensibility. By wit, a well-organised evasiveness, and a preference for the artificial, Hockney manages a breakthrough into creativity."[55]

Although the aesthetic merit of Hazan's film may be more tenuous, it is clear that he wanted to tease out the implications of Hockney's work—namely, to highlight the performative aspects of Hockney's attempts to construct a persona for himself using both painterly and theatrical elements. When Hockney first moved to Los Angeles, he dyed his hair as light as possible and began to dress like one of his paintings by wearing socks of different shades of primary color or contrasting patterned shirts and bow ties that often balance each other as if part of a painterly composition. Mirroring Warhol's own fright-shock wigs and huge eyeglasses, Hockney's performance of self is part and parcel of his paintings, his autobiographical memoirs, and his sense that the artificiality of Southern California begs for just such a reinvention of oneself.

Though certainly not the only artist to create himself as a work of art, Hockney can be said to represent an entire generation of gay, lesbian, and bisexual artists for whom this self-creation denotes a genuinely queer practice. That the era of hyperconsumption that began with the 1960s only enticed and strengthened this connection by adding the element of consumerism is clear in the work of Warhol especially. The movies of John Waters, as well as the work of younger queer writers and directors, are examples of the continuation of this sensibility.

Forced into exile or, if trapped in suburbia, toward a nonqueer life that might be worse, many of these artists may have seen the wedding of performance with art (or writing) as a way to escape or overcome psychologically the life that they would be forced into should they renounce or suppress their sexuality. That this acting out should create a tendency toward the camp or queer as an aesthetic sensibility has been much remarked on. That this lineage should also be a part of larger patterns of cultural production—avant-gardist, performative in a variety of ways, modernist and postmodernist alike—has really only been hinted at. That a queer sensibility is at the heart of much of what we consider artistically transgressive can be taken as a given, but that gay cultural production of some sort can also be taken as a part of a much more accepted tradition should also be understood as well.

CHAPTER 5

Phenomenology of Performance:
David Bowie

Politics of Sound

In 1958 Allan Kaprow, the inventor of the "Happening," called for the creation of a total art form. Citing Wagner and the symbolist poets, Kaprow outlined as the first principle that "the line between the Happening and daily life should be kept as fluid and perhaps indistinct as possible."[1] Basing his work on Goffman's influential *Presentation of Self in Everyday Life* (1959), Kaprow's insistence on "performing life" was in many ways a precursor to the direction David Bowie would take in the 1970s. Along with Capote, Warhol, and Hockney, Bowie represents contemporary culture as a heterogeneous expression of a performative self and acts as the ultimate type of Wilde in his ability to take Wilde's permutations and transformations of self and fashion a career that is based completely on displaying and practicing this performative paradigm. Whereas both Capote and Warhol cling to an idea that they are artists, Bowie goes further in abandoning the dictates of his medium to fashion experimental work from within a genre.

Bowie's unique abilities were first realized in his successful transformation into Ziggy Stardust via exposure to Warhol's *Pork*[2]—a theater piece that may well have galvanized many of the tendencies in Bowie's performance, linking the perverse desire of Ziggy to the theatrical aura Bowie was already developing through mime and other interactive art forms. Certainly Bowie was impressed with Warhol then and now, having penned a song about him for his second major album, *Hunky Dory* (1971), and later playing him in the film *Basquiat* (1996). Bowie's earlier exposure to the U.S. version of art rock—in the form of Warhol's Velvet Underground—was buttressed by years in the British version of the same: the art students who became rockers out of default more than from a desire to choose music over any other medium of expression.[3] After flirting with styles of authenticity on *Hunky Dory* (including an homage to Dylan), Bowie quickly established himself and his songs as anti-sixties, pro-seventies anthems for the doomed youth of the future. Bowie's famed artificiality sprang from a desire to reject the immediate history of rock music. By appearing as Ziggy Stardust, he not only created his most famous character but also (re)launched his career in such a way that he freed himself from the hippie tradition of rock. What became clear with Ziggy was that he had created his own genre of rock music by breaking not some but almost all the rules of rock performance. Indeed, throughout the seventies, Bowie never let the radical members of his audience down as he continually metamorphosed into a succession of ever more literal—and politically astute—personae, even as he also became more and more cerebrally experimental. In a career rare in popular culture, Bowie became commercially successful precisely by allowing himself to become artistically vanguard, even alienating, to the very middle-class fans who formed the base of his fame.[4] His recordings showed a remarkable range of experimentation as he reformed his aesthetic with each album, not always remaining particularly consistent even within one project. Bowie often seemed to jump from one musical style to another, with sometimes two or more overlapping on one album. Compounding this already barely linear career was Bowie's steadfastly "aestheticist" approach to songwriting, one in which he layered irony on irony and image on image in much of his music—including both obscure personal references and references that were just plain obscure, such as those to the Kabbalah in his popular song "Station to Station."

Stealing—or learning—from sources that range from Cage and Glass to Anthony Newley and sixties jazz bands, Bowie was able to fuse disparate elements. Though spawning some of the worst groups of the eighties as he came out of the unsettling, overproduced music scene in the seventies, Bowie was himself—ironically—the real thing. By 1983, with his first international hit album, *Let's Dance*, he finally passed from the status of rock eccentric to rock classic. He became an accepted and acknowledged source of inspiration—a major stylist—on a par with other legendary names of his own generation. This transformation of his reception was actually a long time coming but testifies to his ability to weave experimentation and popularity into financial success.

Twilight Parties

> I made him look me in the eyes and asked him if he would still love me if I told him I wasn't who I'd claimed to be, if I looked just like someone else, if I'd kept my face but changed my name, if I had been quoting someone else when I whispered in his ear.

—Neil Bartlett

In a recent interview for *Out* magazine, Bowie argues that "ambiguity" should not be used as a word to describe his bisexual identity in the seventies: "I was fairly forthcoming about the fact that I was bisexual. I don't think there was any question of me being ambiguous, was there? I think Ziggy was ambiguous, but not me personally."[5] Bowie's changing responses to the perennial questions about his professed sexuality then, his apparent sexuality now, and his influences as a symbol of sexual allusiveness have often been ones to which he reacts with some impatience. Claiming to be gay in the famous *Melody Maker* interview of January 1972, he also granted several interviews with the gay magazine *Jeremy* in 1970. This almost unprecedented embracing of the sexual underground at the time was as responsible for Bowie's influence on sexuality as his subsequent gender-bending styles. As late as 1976, he was still proclaiming in print that he was bisexual, though in the 1980s, with the advent of his first major commercial success, Bowie distanced himself from his earlier claims. Though not now a practicing gay man, Bowie has still been one of the most influential forces for the shaping of queer iconography within popular culture. In the same interview in *Out*, Bowie mentions Brett Anderson and the late Kurt Cobain as inspirations for a song on his new album entitled "Hallo Spaceboy," which contains the lyrics "Do you like girls or boys? / It's confusing these days." Bowie acknowledges here his own importance as a key figure who helped to link underground gay culture to the avant-garde, which is one of the reasons he has been treated as the primary ancestor for the current period of "alternative" music, when many performers—the lead singers of Green Day and REM, for instance—are calling themselves bisexual and younger fans are attaching "alt." culture to queer poses, looks, fashions, and desires.[6]

Around 1972 Bowie's performances began to make visible the erotic energy that was contained in rock music that was not until then directly represented as gay or lesbian. Bowie's own movement in this direction was an inevitable outgrowth of his major intellectual influence: Lindsay Kemp, a Scottish mime who was both extravagantly "out" as well as highly inventive at combining avant-garde art forms with gay self-expression. Along with training in mime, acting, dance, and Asian philosophy, Kemp afforded Bowie with a connection to seventies queer culture—an indebtedness he can never escape, as both what he learned from Kemp and what he was experiencing via his own sexuality at this time were to have profound influences on his subsequent performance style. Just as Newton Arvin had, as lover and teacher, acted as Capote's primary intellectual mentor, Kemp put Bowie in tune with intellectual ideas that he was to build on. The "decadent" seriousness of Kemp's work helped Bowie fashion a career of ironizing detachment. In 1968 Bowie appeared with the Lindsay Kemp Theatre Group as the character Cloud in the production *Pierrot in Turquoise*, which was written and directed by Kemp, with songs written by Bowie that were well received at the time. By 1972 Bowie's Ziggy Stardust concerts at the Rainbow theater in London were extravagant testaments to his own ability to combine mime, theater, and music to create a performance experience unlike any seen before. Bowie invited Kemp to perform with him there, in part to thank him for his earlier influence. Indeed, his use of sexual imagery as Ziggy owed much to Kemp's own performance style, an example of which can be seen in Derek Jarman's 1976 film *Sebastiane*—perhaps the only movie ever to be written in Latin.[7] In an article on Kemp written by Jarman several years after the film, Jarman notes that Kemp "was able to integrate all the diverse elements of design, dance and theatre into a new and exciting unity that in fact has very ancient roots in European theatre, going back to the tradition of the Comedia dell'Arte. His performance art also links up with traditions and developments to be found in Japanese theatre."[8] Jarman goes on to cite Hockney as "one of the first openly gay artists to help change the intellectual climate toward homosexuality in the art world. What David Hockney did for the art world Lindsay did for the theatre."[9]

When Bowie's career began, the multiple permutations that are often associated with him, from Ziggy Stardust to Halloween Jack and beyond, were already there in the numerous bands that he would form—the Lower Third, the King Bees, the Manish Boys—only to disband because of financial reasons. With each new attempt to break into pop's mainstream, he reconceptualized his band as something he had never tried: rhythm and blues, jazz, and so forth. It was as easy for Bowie to absorb new musical styles—and master them—as not to. Indeed, reflecting influences as he was exposed to them was simply how he worked. His own desire to make money and be a success, however, was obviously the medium through which the subcultural strata that he mined were created and made available in late-sixties London. Bowie's commercialism—donning a style as if it were a hat—was a part of his modus operandi from the beginning of his career.[10] This very ability to transform himself was, of course, what made him also disrupt the cardinal rule of American versions of rock: the primary directive that states you find a style and stick with it, as this is not only safe but what your fans expect. Rock, as a testament to faith, was not what Bowie was about.

Bowie's early days as a serious performer with Kemp's company were made easier by the fact that he felt more comfortable performing live when he could hide behind a character. That is, Bowie was extremely frightened by the idea of performing in public, and when it came to performing his songs by himself, he fell back on what he had liked about mime: the singer could hide behind a character in the same way that a mime could hide behind his mask. Bowie transposed the convention of one ancient art form onto a relatively new one. Though he was hardly the first rock performer either to don a character or to make an audience self-conscious about the artificiality of the medium—one need only think of precursors such as Debbie Gore and Little Richard— Bowie did make his absorption into a character much more theatrical than perhaps any rock performer up until that time. Bowie's earliest solo performances of his work after Kemp were marked, then, by the attention to the creation of a character in an attempt simply to get himself through his performances. What Bowie discovered once he got used to this process was that he not only felt comfortable performing in this way but was good at it.

In an early attempt to create a short film of what would now be called promotional videos—*Love You 'Til Tuesday*[11]—Bowie included a short sketch scripted by him entitled "The Mask (A Mime)." Combining voice-over narration with pantomime, Bowie tells the story of a young man who becomes a popular actor when he finds a mask in an antique shop in London. The mask gives him the power to perform until one night onstage he suffocates and dies. The piece ends with the narrator noting, "Funny, though, they [the papers] didn't mention *anything* about a mask." The seventies were for Bowie a time in which he always wore a mask and seemed afraid to take it off lest his fame fade. Unlike the variation on this parable found in Ingmar Bergman's *Persona* (1966), Bowie failed to fall mute, though he did ultimately have a series of breakdowns that removed him from the high life of Los Angeles to the low life of Berlin—a city whose fractured nature became emblematic for him of his own life and, with a failed "bisexual" marriage to U.S. model Angela Barnett, helped him to restructure his psyche. Though it would still be several years before he would completely abandon characters, he never returned to them with the same intensity he had shown from his early British period through his success in the mid-seventies.[12]

However, Bowie's style of performance did in many ways retain the traits that he developed at an early age under the tutelage of Kemp. Already in the clips that make up *Love You 'Til Tuesday*, most of Bowie's gestural performance style is in place. That is, Bowie's style of acting was already characterized by an economy of gesture that was learned from a combination of mime and other gestural vocabularies drawn from film, the stage, and other rock singers. For Ziggy Stardust, Bowie displayed bits of characteristics he garnered from Kemp's own theatricality as well as the London gay world in general, crossed with the working-class grit of glam-rock pioneer Marc Bolan. For the somewhat more ethereal Aladdin Sane, Bowie came closest to camp, though he was also, in 1973, influenced by the Stones. For Halloween Jack of the *Diamond Dogs* album (1984) and tour, he used much more theatricalized singing that, though nominally told through one character's voice, really was an amalgam of voices and characters, as the album had originally been planned as a sort of rock opera/performance piece based on *1984*. In each of these instances, Bowie's performance was devoutly stylized. Indeed, while Bowie frequently references the Pierrot figure in his music—most dramatically on the album and sleeve covers of *Scary Monsters* (1980), where he is dressed as a "white clown"—he is often referencing Asian traditions as well. By using only a few ingredients, Bowie is able not only to be economical but also to make clear to his audience—whether on film or video or in concert—that he is in fact performing a performance: that, as in Japanese drama especially, what one is seeing is to be thought of not as real but as staged and artificial—that is, as a performance to be deconstructed.

Along with the influence of Lindsay Kemp, of the many other obvious influences in Bowie's early-seventies work—Nietzsche, Kubrick, Burroughs, Rechy,[13] science fiction, Weimar German decadence, gay culture generally—"Oriental" style and design were the most important. Like Wilde, Bowie associated the Oriental with an ability to present androgyny as a hyperstylization that draws on transgressive fantasies of bi- or unisexed beings. Bowie's most literal example of this influence was in the clothes created for him by Japanese designer Kansai Yamamoto, who designed futuristic Asian-styled costumes for the Ziggy Stardust tour. The most expensive costumes of this era (one costume alone cost $350,000), the spidery, semisheer fabric emphasized Bowie's delicacy and androgyny.[14] Indeed, Bowie's use of costume at this time often meant taking the sartorial excesses of seventies clothing—platform shoes, mixed patterns, artificial fabrics—and sending them up with sci-fi, gender-bending touches resulting in extremely ugly creations that could never-theless be compoundingly erotic in their ingenious display of his skin. The designs often emphasized his long legs, his shoulders, and his stomach: areas usually associated with the male gaze of a woman's body. This feminizing effect was reflected in the glitter of the costumes, which signified both glamour and the feminine as excess. While Ziggy/Bowie's snow-white skin and powdered face might seem an unerotic surface—a mask on which to paint "emotion"—the costume designers placed fur or fringe along the seam where Bowie's flesh met fabric, creating a highly charged frisson while also dividing his body into a series of erogenous zones that were expertly framed by Bowie in the var-ious poses and positions that he assumed during performance.[15] Indeed, much of what might be seen as Bowie's ability to create—or draw from—a gay erotics came from his ability to suggest (better than a tal-ented transvestite) how the body in its clothes codes gender and encodes sexuality.[16] The constantly shifting signals—somewhat macho in this song, with the crotch emphasized; feminine and vulnerable in this one; outright gay while pantomiming fellatio on Mick Ronson—allowed Bowie in his performances as Ziggy Stardust and other seventies char-acters to go further than anyone in rock music probably ever has at effectively questioning the performer's role as a sexual being. If the audience for a rock concert is supposed to identify with the star—or his persona—as Bowie's obviously do, then the fans, too, question and act out similar dissections of sexual and gender construction by identifying with Bowie's performance. It is in this way that Bowie's famous gender bending can be seen as subversive or liberating. As John Gill notes in *Queer Noises*:

As someone who left school aged fifteen, the year David Bowie released *Hunky Dory*, I belong to a generation that probably has to thank Queer David for the comparative ease with which we came out. However outrageous the model, Queer David was blessed with the glow of celebrity . . . at a time when queer appearances in the media tended to be in the form of arrests and police statistics.[17]

Though Gill goes on to criticize Bowie for not maintaining his sexual subversiveness into his middle age, he does point out that Bowie's significance to a generation is important as a liberatory example: "Michel Foucault would probably disapprove, but Queer David's . . . packaging of sexual outrage created a safe space where many of us, gay, bi, or straight, could play out games and experiment with difference, finding

David Bowie as Ziggy Stardust.

ourselves and going through the motions of teenage rebellion, in a way that not even punk could imitate."[18] Kemp's combining of openly queer erotics, stylized Asian theater techniques, and attention to costume design created for Jarman the "strong visual images" that he was to take away from Kemp's performances.[19] A similar performance style was to form a large part of Bowie's own stage appeal.

In a discussion of the aesthetics of rock and roll, Theodore Gracyk posits "performance" as a key term, as he sees rock music as breaking with jazz, folk, classical, and country in its refusal to provide "realism" or "fidelity to performance" and to see "recording" as the performance itself.[20] Live performance therefore further complicates the formula. As the original work is already "virtual," the text's reproduction, which must be somewhat faithful, is of a work that already exists only as a simulacrum—or as a contentless performance whose text is nonexistent except in the final studio product. We can say, then, that most of the creativity goes into the studio process, not in the repetition of concert performances.[21] As Simon Frith asks, "What would it mean to treat popular musicians as performance artists?"[22] Frith argues:

> The term performance is a form of rhetoric, a rhetoric of gestures in which, by and large, bodily movements and signs (including the use of the voice) dominate other forms of communicative signs, such as language and iconography. And such a use of the body (which is obviously central to what's meant here by performance art) depends on the audience's ability to understand it both as an object (an erotic object, an attractive object, a repulsive object, a social object) and as a subject, that is, as a willed or shaped object, an object with meaning. Rhetorically, then, performance art is a way not of acting but of posing: it takes for granted an audience's ability to refer these bodily movements to others.[23]

In an effort to make his music seem visual, Bowie attempted to find corollaries and analogues in sound for the visual and performative aspects he was able to demonstrate live onstage or on video and film. Yet discussing his work in this area is of necessity difficult. As Gaines notes,

"Sound, that elusive signifier, has historically presented a problem for aesthetic theory. . . . In cultural studies, one hears a frequent lament that sound has been incompletely grasped and undertheorized, especially in comparison with the sophisticated and abundant work on the photographic image produced since the seventies."[24] Indeed, at least for work in cultural studies, a useful theorization of the voice is still forthcoming. Though Susan McClary has shown that an understanding of musicology provides one with technical tools,[25] the model that is still most useful for cultural analysis is perhaps Roland Barthes's famous definition for the grain of the voice, which he produced more than twenty years ago: "It is this displacement that I want to outline, not with regard to the whole of music but simply a part of vocal music (lied or *mélodie*): the very precise space (genre) . . . the *grain*, the grain of the voice when the latter is in a dual posture, a dual production—of language and of music."[26] An application of Barthes's description if translated to rock music might sound like Paul Willis's description of rock music's vocal stylings in general: "The sound of a voice and all the extra-linguistic devices used by singers, such as vocal inflections, nuances, hesitations, emphases or sighs, are just as important in conveying meaning as explicit statements, messages and stories."[27] Indeed, these formulations are helpful in beginning to suggest the quick, subtle shifts in tone—from operatic to sincere, parodic to pop—with which Bowie calls attention to his voice in his singing. But though the voice can itself be used as an instrument, what most distinguishes Bowie's singing on his records is not his manipulation of notes but his manipulation of his voice in relation to other sounds. In analyzing Bowie's singing on *Hunky Dory*, the eminent Wilfred Mellors chooses to describe it in what Elizabeth Thomson and David Gutman call the "equation of song-as-performance equals song-as-composition."[28] That is, part of the grain of Bowie's voice is the way in which the performance—often a complex mixture of singing styles, atonal sounds, unorthodox shifts in chords, and speaking—is part of an ensemble not easily discussed in traditional musical terms. The Anthony Newley vibrato, the cabaret-style Tim Curry-ish-ness of Bowie's vocal performance—throaty and powerful, especially in some of his early records—is distinctive of a type of singing that almost oversignifies to remind listeners repeatedly that what they are hearing is a self-conscious performance of character and emotion (singing to make you think about singing) that yet connects to many people because it is closer to how they experience emotion than music that attempts to be "naturalistic." Bowie's vocal performances bespeak the realm of queer vocal erotics.

Indeed, perhaps this artificiality in Bowie's vocal performance is most important to note in his falsetto singing, which appears throughout his recordings. Though one may wish to theorize this type of singing as signifying as "queer" in its ability to create a disjunction between the male singer and the supposedly naturalizing signification of a "normal" male voice—a gender dysfunction that can be used to create an unreal sound, from country yodeling to the crooning of Prince and Aaron Neville—Bowie's falsetto usually works to create a momentary change in chord or tempo, rather than to signify queerly the way it does for someone like Little Richard. The liberal use that Bowie makes of falsetto, however, seems to suggest that he was, like other queer singers, not at all afraid to use it. Sometimes, as in his duet with Tina Turner on his remake of "Tonight," the higher octave range is a bit destabilizing in terms of gender because it may well constitute the range where his voice sounds its most melodic. Yet in addition to using his voice to reach a higher octave, he often creates the same effect using electronic treatments to extend his range into the upper reaches. The most famous example of this is the stunning reverse crescendo at the end of "Fame." Indeed, he altered his voice electronically on some of his music as early as the sixties. By the late seventies, Bowie used not only the vocoder but many versions of this synthesized voice for *Scary Monsters*, which suggests the extent to which he was influenced by electronic German groups such as Kraftwerk. Performance artist Laurie Anderson, who used similar synthesized voices extensively in her massive tour United States I–IV, must surely have been aware of experiments on Bowie's part, especially in her use of the digital synthesizer to lower her voice to create a male alter ego to perform onstage during portions of her concert. Bowie's use of falsetto, though an example of queer erotics at work, is also an example of the way in which his voice has been used like his stage work to take a queerly marked concept and use it to various ends in a variety of contexts.

In a discussion of the career of Bryan Ferry, one of the few genuine colleagues that Bowie has, Ian Penman describes Ferry's voice as "an *autographic* voice, signing in the register of song, under an assumed name or an adoptive one: this, for the time being, is his [Ferry's] style."[29] Bowie's mode of singing is similarly marked as signed and, especially, authorized by him. Unlike Ferry, however, Bowie's inflections in his singing and differences in his production do not work to move him toward any one thing but rather change with each album—sometimes with each song—to produce not a perfectly running, always-recognizable song styling as in the work of Ferry but an approach to singing that aims to destabilize one's ideas about what constitutes singing even as an always-recognizable approach to singing (if only in the self-referencing) is always clearly present. Bowie's singing does much the same work as his other performances and is probably the basis for all of the others, as Bowie attempts to be romantic not only in terms of his many personae and his practice of life as art but also in his emphasis on art as becoming, not being, irony rather than sentimentalization.

Bodies of Desire: *Merry Christmas, Mr. Lawrence*

An example of how Bowie was able to translate the performative style embedded in his music to various visual media can be seen in his starring role in the film *Merry Christmas, Mr. Lawrence* (1983). The idealized identification that the fan has for the rock star as it appears in many of Bowie's songs is used by Nagisa Oshima to explore the conflicted symbiotic relationship between viewer and film, West and East, during a period of stress and rupture. Taking place near the end of World War II, the film is set in a Japanese prison camp in Malta. Bowie plays a war hero who is brought to the camp, only to become the erotic fixation of the camp's young commander, played by Bowie's Japanese counterpart in real life, rock star Ryuichi Sakamoto. The film's exploration of same-sex desire is magnified and intertwined with the idea of race as the homoerotic "other" of attraction between the prisoners. Oshima emphasizes this intercultural theme in the casting of Tom Conti and "Beat" Takeshi as Bowie's and Sakamoto's confidants, respectively. While Conti and Takeshi come out of acting traditions that are more conventional for their respective cultures, Bowie and Sakamoto were chosen self-consciously by Oshima precisely because they are not playing from any kind of "naturalistic" or method school. Bowie's concise gestural style of acting is used by Oshima to straddle the cultural and sexual gray zones that the film explores. Serving in his own way as an ambassador of East and West, Bowie's performance is a virtuoso example of a style of acting that is based on Brechtian theories.

The film was released in the same year as *Let's Dance*, and the theme of Bowie's subsequent world tour was a sort of quasi-Asian port motif, with Bowie appearing much as he does in the film. In a sense, Bowie plays the same character he developed for the stage, which seems to be based on the album's song "China Girl," when the singer croons to his lover: "I'll give you eyes of blue / I'll give you man who wants to rule the world." Bowie is the white man cometh who is, in the film, everything the Japanese commander wants.[30] The one person he is supposed to hate the most, in other words, is also the object of his affection.

By using rock stars, Oshima's gambit was that he could bring a version of stylized—that is, Orientalized—acting to the representation of homosexual passion. If Oshima's experiment was to be successful, Bowie and Sakamoto had to be believable not only as performers but also as actors. Owing mostly to his disciplined performance, Bowie especially was able to deliver the effect that Oshima wanted by creating his character primarily through gesture and very slight facial expression, much like his performances in rock concerts and in music videos. For example, shortly after his arrival at the camp, Celliers prepares to be carried away to be executed by a firing squad in what turns out to be a form of psychological torture—the guns fire blanks. Before leaving for what he thinks is his death, Bowie's character mimes a quick shave and cigarette. This bit of theatricality was suggested by Bowie and displays much of the technique used by him to express his laconic character's emotions and attitude throughout the film.[31] At the end, as Yanoi begins the ritual execution of one of the British officers, Celliers/Bowie breaks ranks, walks up to Yanoi/Sakamoto, and kisses him stiffly on the cheek. Sakamoto swoons and falls to the ground to the strains of his own rapturous instrumental sound track. The single gesture of the kiss, therefore, is all the more powerful because we the audience know by then what gestures mean to this character—and how he understands their symbolic importance to the Japanese culture in which he finds himself. Using a stylized code, Celliers is able to communicate with people whom he not only loathes, but with whom he cannot communicate verbally. Bowie and Oshima use the kiss as the way for Celliers to indicate that he understands the commander's love and is willing to acknowledge it, just as the mime shows his initial defiance of the prison's control.

In a discussion of Brecht's requirement that epic theater "frame *within* the frame," John Mowitt notes that "the frame *makes* a difference. Would it not be possible to see Benjamin's stylistic investment in the aphorism as an expression of this state of affairs? I am thinking here . . .

Bowie plants a kiss in *Merry Christmas, Mr. Lawrence.*

of the aphorism's . . . abrupt concision of its style."[32] Indeed, one could describe Bowie's performance in the film as a form of visual aphorism. Bowie makes the audience conscious that what they are seeing is not realistic acting. At the same time, the ability to quote—to use the visual in a textual way—allows him to comment on the very techniques that go into assembling the illusion of a character on the screen.[33] Just as Brecht and Artaud wanted their actors either to escape the proscenium arch or at least to make the audience aware that what is within it is not real, so Bowie, drawing on Japanese tradition, makes the audience aware that his performance is a series of quasi-illusory masks—or rather, as in Noh, one blank mask on which emotions are read not via changes in the mask's surface but by modulations in the body's gestures and the sets, light, music, and noise around him. Bowie uses the techniques from Kemp to create a version of his current rock persona to flesh out a film character for a major international director. In this sense, then, Bowie is actually framing performance itself as the art form that he uses: the transformation of self into a template that can be used to write any number of characters, stories, and emotions—or fragments of all three.

"Stylistic gesture," as Bowie calls it, is an attempt to create emotion in the audience as opposed to drawing "the audience into the emotional content of what you're doing."[34] Bowie's performance, considered by some critics to be the best of his career, is central to understanding a film that uses its own self-reflexiveness as a commentary on the vicissitudes of life during wartime. Bowie's and Sakamoto's characters, each in his own way, are haunted by questions of honor and duty. Oshima uses the spectacle of Bowie's body—most especially his (then) blond hair and tan face—as a stylized symbol of Western beauty and cultural fetishism: an unattainable object that becomes a field of conflicting desires. By playing down the individuality of his own Western subject position, Bowie allows the film to examine the realm of subject/object tension that Oshima seems to posit as central to the mutual coexistence of Eastern and Western cultural positions. Ultimately the film is itself a utopian gesture that calls into question whether difference (culture) or sameness (gender/sex) dictates the vicissitudes of desire.

Dramatis Personae: *Video Work*

> What people call insincerity is simply a method by which we can
> multiply our personalities.
>
> —Wilde, "The Critic as Artist"

> I consider myself responsible for a whole new school of pretensions.
>
> —Bowie

"The mums and dads thought I was weird, but I'm not an innovator.
I'm really just a photostat machine," Bowie proclaimed in an interview
published in 1973. Indeed, his ability to change from Major Tom to a
"leper messiah" was, he has claimed, more his reflection of the milieu
and times in which he found himself than the refinement—or play
with—a stable, central self. Bowie's seeming abandonment of his ego—
or willingness to subordinate it—has much to do with his belief in an
Eastern approach to will. Treating himself along the lines of the Bud-
dhist concept of the hollow vessel waiting to be filled, Bowie claims that
his music is made up of a pastiche of found lyrics, characters, and sounds
because it is the scavenging of cultures and Zeitgeists that forms each
successive musical and character change for each new album. Of course,
it is also quite possible to think that Bowie's changes have as much to
do with canny commerce. As he himself has admitted, commerce is what
drives him as much as anything else. What he does not usually discuss
is his amazing ability to create synergistic media campaigns for each
album. Beginning with his early successes, Bowie not only referred to
himself as "The Actor" but also hired actual actors to staff his office.[35]
Though this was hardly efficient, it points up Bowie's efforts to merge
art with life. Beyond simply being Ziggy offstage, Bowie wanted to make
the character/concept so enticing that all aspects of his performance—
singing, stage appearances, interviews, travel, work, and play in toto—
could be seen as one seamless, constructed whole. Rather than merely
one complex artistic concept, however, Bowie's synergy was also one
gigantic money machine. Bowie harnessed the artistic process itself to

capitalism in its purest form: breaking down the barriers between the different frontiers—the different ways of making money—so that they could feed on each other. In this way, the profits are maximized. Bowie became his own oligarchy.

Bowie's promotional videos for his various albums provide perhaps the best example of his abilities at combining art and commerce. Though Bowie's own concerts often play on or seem to reference the performance artists of the day—as can be seen in his collaborations with Robert Wilson, Pina Bausch, Ton Basil, LaLaLa Human Steps, and others—his videos represent a medium that he himself helped to fashion. If Bowie's concerts often seemed to involve a "debasing" of ideas and concepts from performance artists, his work in video represented his ability to take television and make of it a "high" art experience by the sheer brilliance with which he expanded the vocabulary of the genre. Although, as J. Hoberman notes, like most video pioneers Bowie borrowed from other sources—avant-garde films, painting, and so forth—to create some of his video effects, in many important ways Bowie's forays into this medium increasingly represented the source of his characters and performance—especially from 1979 until the mid-eighties. During this period, videos represented his most sustained effort at marketing himself and especially at creating an image or character that was meant not only to complement his music but, in some instances, to provide both a critique of it and a fuller autobiographical statement of what he was attempting to do in his work as a whole. Combining as they do the visual with acting and music, music videos have provided Bowie with some of his most ironic and interesting work to date.

Indeed, from his first forays into video, Bowie used the form not merely as a promotional clip but also as a way to expand or redefine the characters referenced in his songs. For example, in the clip prepared for "John, I'm Only Dancing," Bowie appears in a black leather jacket with an anchor tattooed on his right cheek in an obvious attempt at a gay type. The song, which Bowie has released in at least five different versions, is a tongue-in-cheek plea sung by a gay man to his lover, asking him not to get angry that he is dancing with a woman because, after all, he is "only dancing," though he does admit that "she turns me on." Sung in a mock wail, Bowie's song could easily be one of the first rock compositions ever to make clear that the singer's persona is that of a gay man. Throughout the video, Bowie caresses his neck and flares his eyes as the song alternates between erotic desire and subtle confrontation, respectively. Crosscut with Bowie and his band are two dancers— one male, and looking much like Kemp himself, the other female. The spidery costumes and choreography, while echoing the song, also emphasize its basic message of emotional entangledness.[36]

Throughout the seventies, Bowie was to continue to allow his videos to comment on his songs in somewhat indirect ways. For example, in his video for "Look Back in Anger" (1979), Bowie plays the character of a poor artist alone in a garret studio, caressing a self-portrait of himself as an angel. As he rubs his hand across the surface, paint appears on his face, which soon looks grotesque—even diseased. As a comment on *Dorian Gray*, Bowie seems to play the parts of both Basil and Dorian—or, indeed, to reinterpret the novel's theme of duality in such a way as to combine the artist with his subject. Bowie here makes his

Bowie in "Look Back in Anger."

most direct homage to Wilde and also joins a tradition of musicians—the Rolling Stones, Morrisey—who also make explicit references to Wilde in this medium. "Look Back in Anger" also sets up the themes for several of Bowie's next clips, most of which deal with the relationship of the artist to his work, such as "DJ" (1979) and "Ashes to Ashes" (1980), the latter bringing an ambiguous closure to his video performances from that decade.

Made as a commercial for his album *Lodger*, the title "DJ" may well be an autobiographical reference to Bowie's given name, David Jones, but in this video the character portrayed is not a painter but someone who selects from others' music—a disc jockey who proclaims, "I am what I play." The video crosscuts between the interior of a radio station to a scene of Bowie walking along a sidewalk in London. Two men and a woman stop to kiss him. He carries the men along with him on his arm. These scenes seem to echo the song's reference to "believers believing me." That is, the events on the street prove his fame, though the homoerotic appeal of much of it seems to echo the song's opening remarks about having a girlfriend who is dancing. Seemingly a reference to the gay speaker of "John, I'm Only Dancing," it may well be that Bowie's situation is reversed here, as it may be the girlfriend who is dancing without him, and presumably with another woman. Released around the time of his breakup with his bisexual wife Angie Bowie, the tense fragility of the lyrics may represent the darker times of his own personal relationships.

Entitled "Boys Keep Swinging," Bowie's third video from a song on the album *Lodger* was not a paean to fond memories of boyhood—as its jaunty lyrics might suggest on an initial hearing—but rather an indictment of male privilege: "When you're a boy / You can wear a uniform / When you're a boy / Other boys check you out." The lyrics catalog a series of acquisitive pleasures that might seem uniquely masculine, sung against a musical background whose sinister grind sounds as if it is about to break apart. Indeed, the Eno-processed song was recorded using instructions that Eno turned up randomly from a special deck of tarotlike cards. One of the results of using this method to construct the song was to have all the recording musicians switch instruments. Quite literally, the music is a fragile "medley" of sounds—some innovative and some simply dissonant. Bowie's album—one of his most political—was to give the lie to the idea that his music up until then had been apolitical, as some on the left have claimed.[37] The album's politics concern gender inequity. The penultimate song, "Repetition," deals quite realistically with wife battering, and the album's first song, "Fantastic Voyage," is a plea for nuclear disarmament. One of his most influential videos, "Boys Keep Swinging," opens with Bowie singing in what appears to be regular street clothes—a coat and loosened tie. During the song's chorus, he appears as three different female stars as he walks out onto a catwalk—Lauren Bacall, British TV personality Bet Lynch, and Marlene Dietrich. Twice he removes his wig and smears his makeup across his face—violent gestures that are particularly unsettling when performed with the jarring, discordant music. Though filmed as if it were a drag show—with Bowie playing all the parts—the video is a satire on drag or rather references the specific drag act of Rommy Haag to make a point not only about male privilege but also about the assumptions behind men using systems of signification that code them as "female," no matter how ironizing the performance might be. Bowie is not attempting merely to shock bourgeois sensibility. Rather, he uses elements from underground gay culture to broach debates about how gender and sexuality function to define artistic expression. His attention on *Lodger* to the specific politics of feminist critiques of the patriarchal system and its violence against women does not place his work in this video in the realm of camp aesthetics but allies it instead with feminist video work. The performance provides a stinging critique of the song's lyrics, purposefully shutting down some "innocent" interpretations for one that is much more pointedly political. That is, Bowie acknowledges and comments on the fact of male privilege and that gender is not just an act to be performed. His understanding of the potentialities of the performance of gender in a theatricalized venue had changed and was, more or less, to disappear from his work after his next album, *Scary Monsters (and Super Creeps)*.

With *Scary Monsters*, Bowie created simultaneously his most self-reflexive and schizophrenic album—one that made its politics known up front. The album begins with the female singer Michi Hirota belting out the lyrics to the first song in a Japanese translation. Bowie's intention was to explode the myth of the Asian woman as petite and fragile. The howling vocals of the song are echoed in Robert Fripp's guitar work and reproduced in Bowie's own singing. The pointedness of his lyrics is meant to undercut theatricality in favor of political urgency. In a rare display of sincerity, Bowie even distances himself from his first persona, Major Tom, in the brilliant "Ashes to Ashes." A distillation of the anxiety that went into the preceding Berlin trilogy, the video opens with Bowie in total Pierrot costume referencing the character Major Tom from "Space Oddity," which is immediately followed by Bowie holding up a mirror. The following events of the song seem to take place both within the mirror and on what turns out to be a beach, though one more suggestive of a nuclear waste site rather than the fertility of the ocean. Intercut with Bowie dressed as Pierrot are scenes of Bowie in a

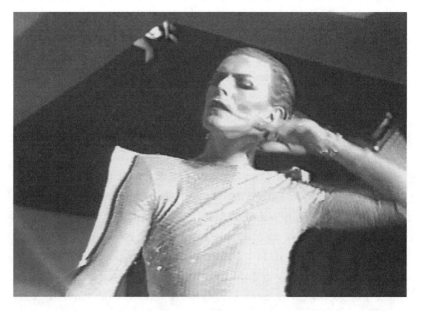

Bowie smearing makeup in "Boys Keep Swinging."

padded cell, strapped to a chair in a 1950s-era kitchen, and attached to a bathysphere underwater—images that magnify the song's lyrics while refusing to explain them. Throughout much of the song, Bowie sings in a neutral, eerily calm voice—as if resigned or coerced into his fate. A perfect video in its ability to create added textures and associations for the song, it ends with Bowie once again as Pierrot walking along the beach accompanied by an actress playing his mother, who also warns against Major Tom.

Bowie was to go on to make many other influential and successful videos that have, in the main, stayed away from the interiority of his production in the seventies. Indeed, when in 1982 he finally made a video for the album *Station to Station*, which had been released in 1976, he based it on black-and-white films of jazz shows that he had seen as a child in London. The videos for *Let's Dance*, with their pointed messages about the mistreatment of minorities in Australia, were apparently meant to reflect a new Bowie reaching outside himself. More recent videos, for *Tonight* and *Black Tie, White Noise*, are balanced between the

Bowie as Pierrot in "Ashes to Ashes."

avant-gardist experimentation of "Ashes to Ashes" and the blatant political message of "China Girl" but still retain self-referential moments—actresses dressed as the flight attendant from *2001: A Space Odyssey* (1968) appear in "They Say Jump" as a sly reference to "Space Oddity"—and an ability to present his music as more than simply a linear melody. When director Gus Van Sant directed Bowie in 1990 for a video of the remake of his Grammy-winning single "Fame," he placed a frame around the border of the screen that was made up of various clips of Bowie performing during different periods. Van Sant seemed to understand that any reference to Bowie now is also to Bowie's many past masks and creations, which always frame his moves.

Bowie's own most dramatic example of this type of self-examination as a performer came in the form of a twenty-minute mini-movie based on one of his songs. *Jazzin' for Blue Jean*, directed by Julien Temple in 1984, was the first long version of a video ever filmed (followed shortly by Michael Jackson's *Thriller*). Temple takes Bowie's short, pithy pop tune "Blue Jean" and gives it not only a new meaning but also a story line and three characters. Bowie plays two parts—the egocentric rock star, Screamin' Lord Byron, and a hapless average guy, Vic, who works down the street from the theater where Lord Byron is scheduled to perform. The third character is a woman who is an avid fan of Lord Byron's and who is enticed into a date with Vic by his promising her he knows Byron: "David Hockney introduced us." We meet Lord Byron as he arrives at the theater on a stretcher with an oxygen mask attached to his face. We next see him down pills in his dressing room as he applies his own makeup and casually paints the makeup mirror. After several painful scenes showing attempts by Vic to impress his date, we finally see the film's main event, the performance of "Blue Jean" by Lord Byron. Coming onstage in a male harem costume, Bowie as Byron also wears elaborate makeup created by a then-revolutionary computer technique that makes his face resemble a glowing topography of colors and textures that works with the costume to present a highly Orientalized effect. Bowie sings the song, the audience swoons, the average guy loses the girl. Byron, however, turns out to be a snob ("It was Monte

Carlo, wasn't it?") and a fake. Vic yells after him, "You conniving, randy, bogus, oriental old queen. Your record sleeves are better than your songs. Car stops, girl gets out, hello, Julien. . . ." Bowie's last line is a comment on his own musical and marketing pretensions that ends with him breaking from character as the fictional world of the movie collapses. Bowie's most sustained attempt at a commentary on the fusion of man and mask, the film ends with a shot through a window whose design suggests prison bars, or perhaps barbed wire.

Hoberman and Andrew Goodwin have both theorized that acting in a musical video may have more to do with the presentation of "personality"—such as a news anchor is supposed to do—than acting such as one sees in a film. Goodwin concludes that though a video's compressed distillation of star quality may lack the character development that one sees in a movie, it might make up for it by the "documentary" intensity of its focus on its subject.[38] Though Bowie perhaps changes the rules of the standard video clip format by coming closer to actually playing characters, his videos do show him constantly commenting on his previous incarnations by creating a different version of himself with each

Bowie in *Blue Jean.*

new video—sometimes even creating one that is different from the one in the song itself. This playing with his own self-reference may have much to do with the way in which he sees himself in relation to history. In an essay entitled "Concerning the Progress of Rock and Roll," Michael Jarrett notes that "the dandy . . . 'appears above all in periods of transition,' which makes me suspect that the nearly simultaneous rise of rock & roll and poststructuralism is symptomatic of a paradigm shift, a fundamental change in the way we approach the materials of the past."[39] Like his predecesors in the last fin de siècle, Bowie attempts to demonstrate that it is only through a process of aestheticization and becoming that one can ever hope to change how one lives. This message—acted out by Bowie during the seventies, in particular—is one that he came partially to disown in the nineties, even as he cashed in on his enormous artistic successes from the 1970s. His many performances of self, therefore, are perhaps most complexly developed in his videos, which allow him to add to, comment on, and obliquely tweak his musical personae.

For the next decade, Bowie was to stumble repeatedly and ultimately turn to some of his old personae for help, only to realize too late that he could not re-create those musical styles without simply appearing to repeat himself for no apparent reason other than a desperate attempt at sales. Having rid himself of the various guises and alter egos of the seventies to embrace what he considered the new persona of "normality" that he was to adopt for the eighties, Bowie only succeeded in setting himself adrift. In terms of gender bending, any number of groups, mainly British, were aping his own personae with abandon—from Culture Club to Haircut 100. There was by the mid-eighties hardly any room for Bowie himself. Yet what had become clear after the success of *Let's Dance* was that he no longer really had to do anything. One advantage of this was Bowie's exploration of traditional acting; one disadvantage was the vacuity of Bowie's ideas about musical performance—a problem from which he did not recover until the nineties.

The nineties did show a return to form for Bowie that he owed at least in part to a further strengthening of his interest in technology. His first solo album of the decade, *Black Tie, White Noise* (1993), was released with an accompanying interactive CD-ROM, *Jump*, made from the video created for the album's song "Jump They Say."[40] Bowie's program places the user in a studio to reassemble the video into as many different versions as one would like. Beginning with the Rykodisc Sound and Vision set and tour from 1990, Bowie also rereleased his previous catalog and made available selected unreleased demos and alternate mixes. Just as *Scary Monsters* emphasized fragmentation as a theme in his life, Bowie's major projects in the nineties offered his fans the ability to assemble and replay his career in whatever form they wished. He has provided all the parts, in other words, for one to assemble as many versions of David Bowie as one would like.

For the advertising campaign for *Lodger* (1979), RCA fashioned the slogan "There's old wave, there's new wave, and there's David Bowie." Bowie seems finally, in the nineties, to take seriously the idea that he is his own "style" of music. In the same year as the release of *Black Tie, White Noise*, Philip Glass composed a symphony based on Bowie's album *Low* (1977) and spoke in interviews about how intricate and surprising the structure of the music was.[41] Indeed, if Bowie's album had been a premonition of Glass's own work, Bowie's work with Tin Machine during the late eighties presaged the entire grunge movement. Similarly, *Lodger*'s drawing on African and Asian rhythms foresaw the interest in Third World music that Paul Simon and David Byrne were to explore, while *Young Americans* (1975) was ahead of the curve on transforming funk into disco. Bowie's most recent attempt to return to his Berlin period suggests that he now wants to be thought of as an artist rather than a popular musician. Never one to handle success well, Bowie seems in his latest manifestation to be once again interested in making serious music rather than attempting another platinum record. His most experimental album, *Outside* (1995), teams him once again with Eno in a series of aural experiments that go beyond those attempted by them in the late seventies—at least in terms of their use of the studio itself as a kind of instrument.

City of Night: *Outside*

Bowie begins *Outside* with a series of dates spoken in an incantatory tone by one of seven characters developed for the album. Time is indeed important here, as Bowie makes clear not just in the first track but in the accompanying booklet written by him. Opening on the scene of an "art-murder," the booklet is putatively a series of diary entries by "Detective Professor" Nathan Adler. The first entry, dated Friday, December 31, 1999, references the end of the millennium and begins the album on the day the murder took place. Adler, a sleuth from England who is funded by a futuristic version of the NEA, is in "Oxford Town, New Jersey," to solve the riddle of the murder of a fourteen-year-old girl whose body has been used to create an artistic statement: her limbs severed and dangling from a spider's web created by the arrangement of her intestines, her mangled corpse has been placed on an ivory shaft. "It was definitely murder—but was it art?" Adler asks as his diaries show his mind shifting back and forth from seventies Berlin to mid-nineties New York City and the "present" of New Jersey. Though Bowie never solves the mystery for the listener, he does pose another one: what will happen at the end of the twentieth century? In a teasing answer to this question, Bowie predicts that the fin de siècle will see a further merging of art with violence that will result in a new genre of artistically committed crimes.[42]

Adler represents Bowie's alter ego—they even share the same birthday—and he fills his diary with notes about the artistic influences that seem reflected in the ritual murder. It soon becomes obvious that these ruminations are Bowie's way of telegraphing the concept for this very conceptually driven creation to his fans. Namely, Adler traces the crime to various performance artists from the seventies, eighties, and nineties. Some of these performers are painters, others are photographers, but most have been associated with some type of body art, installation, or performance that involved the mutilation or ritual scarification/piercing of the artist's or someone else's body.[43] One of these artists, Chris Burden, is mentioned in Bowie's song "Joe the Lion," which was recorded in Berlin in 1977. In fact, the diary entries are usually references either to Berlin in the seventies or to the fictitious town of New Jersey in 1999, with occasional references to performance art in the nineties—mainly to Ron Athey, an HIV-positive artist who was the subject of one of the many NEA "scandals" for a section of his performance that used his own blood and raised the question of the audience's relative safety.[44] Bowie is obviously trying to link the body art performance of the seventies—an outgrowth of Fluxus, Happenings, and the work of Rudolf Schwarzkogler in the sixties—with the various panoptic uses of the "AIDS body" in the eighties and nineties.[45] His point is that the ultimate result of this sort of experimentation, at least from a formal standpoint, must be a form of murder as art.

Though it is not too difficult to find the pop cultural precedents for a concept such as this—the flayed police officer in Jonathan Demme's *Silence of the Lambs* (1991), the entrails hung on lamp shades by the real Jack the Ripper, and any number of science fiction movies or *romans policiers* might provide a similar future-shock atmosphere—Bowie's decision to make this material the basis for an album is unusual. The body as performance is to some extent an outgrowth of Bowie's interest in painting and the visual arts—his own paintings having been on display in a one-man show held in London in 1995. Bowie's obsession with, and expertise in, visual art are reflected in his range of reference in the diaries: from the seventeenth-century Dutch painter Paulus Potter to the equally obscure twentieth-century artist Hermann Nitsch.[46] Perhaps more important, though, the idea of the body as art—even in a victimized form—cannot help but allude to Bowie's performance with his own body. Likewise, the photographs of the characters that accompany the text are of Bowie in various disguises posing as several different ages and sexes. The cumulative effect is to comment on his use of theatrical performance, especially in the Diamond Dogs Tour (1974), and to recast it in this merging of print, sound, and photos.[47] The autobiographical effect, signaled by the mock-diary form and the placing of one of his self-portraits on the album's cover, brings the various elements together into a multimedia package that raises another mystery about just what Bowie the artist is attempting to say about himself and his work.[48]

"I suppose you never can tell what an artist will do once he's peaked," wonders Adler. And indeed it is a safe bet that one is supposed to make the same conclusion about Bowie and the latest phase of his career. *Outside* does take the idea of a "concept album" in a new direction, though one foreseen by his own work.[49] What is different are Bowie's academic references—to Rothko and the architect Philip Johnson, for example—and the sort of pretentiousness on which this is founded. Creating a cast of characters, a futuristic lingo for them to speak, and the skeletal outline of a plot, Bowie's album is a remake of *A Clockwork Orange* for the nineties[50]—or perhaps an adaptation of that book as scored by Brecht and Weill.[51] The various songs themselves, each devised to be spoken by a different character, continue the fusion/funk influence of his previous album but add piano arrangements by Mike Garson, who created a brilliant parody of the "stride" piano playing for *Aladdin Sane*, as well as plenty of eroding electronic noise courtesy of Eno's treatment of various kinds of music and sound. Indeed, after a long hiatus, Bowie has found another way to return to the use of characters and, as the album suggests, to find a way once again to represent desires and actions that are outside the mainstream—hence the album's title. If the result is nothing more than the sum of its parts, the references to Bowie's own interests in the painterly and the electronic still link his production in the last two decades with that of his most prolific period: the 1970s.[52] Acting much as Wilde did to focus and contain many different influences coming from changes in culture and art, Bowie—and his production from that decade—is still underexamined. If, as Bowie claims in interviews for his album, his tendency as an artist has always been to take high-art concepts and materials and apply them to a "lower" form of entertainment,[53] then it is in his refashioning of queer performative styles that his importance lies as a key figure in the transposing of the avant-garde ironies of Schlegel and Wilde from one fin de siècle to another.[54]

The Problems with Camp: *Velvet Goldmine*

In formulating a Wildean paradigm for the twentieth century, it is clear that some figures self-consciously place themselves in a lineage that runs back to Wilde—not only Capote and Bowie but also the performance artists Gilbert and George and various others who have taken up some version of the dandy as signifier. There are other sites of performance, however, that seem to exist in various guises related to Wilde that may not be based on Wilde so much as on a parodic or mystified version of him. Indeed, what is unique about Wilde's performance is that it is not necessarily synonymous with the dandy or other types of camp culture that have arisen in the twentieth century. Toward this end, it is important to note what is and is not a part of the paradigm that Wilde left for others to follow. That is, much of what we think of as similar to Wilde may better be examined as parts of other traditions. On the other hand, much that we now take for granted as part of a general queer milieu of campiness, bohemia, or the like may in fact be traceable to Wilde. The point is that the dandical, postromantic, and queer scenes and influences that are often collapsed under general rubrics of camp or queer culture, decadence or the avant-garde, should be analyzed from a materialist standpoint with distinctions made between them. Wilde's importance to queer culture cannot be underestimated. However, the way in which his work, personae, and influence have been misread or changed must be reexamined. The problem with camp is the problem with discussing the emergence not only of new practices but also of the analysis of old ones that now have long and complicated histories that beg to be explicated and understood. As with other areas of study, however, queer theory must attempt to establish links between phenomena rather than attempt simply to summarize a dense nexus of subcultural practice in one word or concept.

A recent attempt to represent Wilde's influence as a complicated historical moment can be seen in Todd Haynes's film fantasy about David Bowie and Oscar Wilde entitled *Velvet Goldmine* (1998). Covering events from the late 1960s to the early 1980s, the film retells much of Bowie's career while wrapping it in a package that formulates both a mythical origin for the emergence of Bowie as well as a stinging political comment on his seeming abandonment of seventies cultural ideas. Haynes's picture is complex. Portions of the film are presented as dream sequences—or rather, sexual fantasies about singers that could come from the minds of the characters, the director, or a fan. The retelling of Bowie's career through the character of Brian Slade (Jonathan Rhys Meyers) is interwoven with the story of one of those fans, Arthur Stuart (Christian Bale), as his life is shaped by his interest in the figures who made glitter happen. Linking these two strands of the plot is an elaborate homage to *Citizen Kane* (1941) in which Bale's character, as a journalist in 1984, attempts to find out what happened to the youthful Slade after he faked his death onstage. Was he simply killing off his creation, Maxwell Demon (i.e., Ziggy Stardust), or was he exiting from rock performance forever? The search for an answer forces Arthur to confront his own past, when glitter music liberated his sexuality and promised a future alternative to the dystopic eighties in which he now lives and works.

In an interview for the film, Haynes claims that he was "interested in glam rock's flag-waving of artificiality—and there's no more articulate spokesperson for artifice than Oscar Wilde."[55] Within the film's fantasy structure, Haynes posits not just a figurative but also a literal connection between Wilde and the extravagantly bisexual symbol of the "glam rock era," Brian Slade. The film opens in Dublin as a baby is delivered via flying saucer to the doorstep of what will be Wilde's home in Merrion Square. In the film's first few moments, the famously alien aspects of Ziggy Stardust are made real. Attached to the baby's layette is a broach containing a green gem—the color that Wilde considered to be suggestive of decadence. The jewel takes on the powers of a talisman as its movement from character to character causes the actual unfolding of glitter history. About a hundred years after Wilde's death, a mysterious figure, Jack Fairy (Micko Westmoreland), finds the bauble in the dirt of his schoolyard after he is beaten up by his classmates. Many years later, Slade, as a nascent Bowie figure, steals the pendant from Fairy the same night that he makes love both to his future wife (Mandy, really Angie Bowie played by Toni Collette) and to Fairy (also a stand-in for Marc Bolan). Slade steals from most everyone in the film (a frequent comment from Bowie's friends) but will ultimately give the pendant to the one true love of his life, Curt Wild (Iggy Pop as played by Ewan McGregor). Late in the film, Wild passes the pin to the film's narrator, the young reporter Arthur, after a night spent with him. This movement suggests Lacan's version of the purloined letter, in which each character's relationship to the signifying force of Wilde's personality is suggested by his or her position vis-à-vis the otherworldly gem.

Connected to this already dense plot is a general celebration of the seventies as a time of overt sexuality and freedom from gender norms. Bowie is seen as the heir to Wilde, who threw it all away—or rather, became a barometer for the changes in society that necessitated the Thatcher/Reagan era. Haynes's ultimate goal seems to be to provide a core sample of a moment in time before this happened, when history seemed to presage something genuinely new. Haynes sees Bowie as existing in symbolic relation to his age, much as Wilde did his own, but also as having a very different end from Wilde's. Whereas Wilde was unable or unwilling to escape homophobia, Bowie avoids that fate, but only by selling out both himself and the aspirations of an entire generation of gay youth.

During the film's first half, we are treated to a retelling of the unofficial history of Bowie's early career with all the characters acting as stand-ins for real figures in Bowie's life as well as for parallels to the

Jonathan Rhys Meyers as Brian Slade in *Velvet Goldmine*.

major characters in *Citizen Kane*. The film re-creates Bowie in his late-sixties excesses—Veronica Lake hairdo, acoustic guitar, Glastonbury—while under the influence of his first manager, Cecil (Michael Feast), standing in for the real Ken Pitt. Slade later replaces Cecil with the more charismatic and macho Jerry Devine (Eddie Izzard)—aka Tony DeFries. At the height of his fame, we see Slade reproduce the famous kiss between Bowie and Lou Reed—here between Slade and Wild. At this point the film begins to diverge significantly from the facts of Bowie's life in its positing of an actual relationship between Slade and Wild—one that is, for Slade, also highly romantic. Other than the idea that opposites attract, we never really know exactly what Slade himself sees in Wild, though Mandy claims it was the beginning of the end of their relationship, as well as the moment when Slade began to change for the worse. After faking his own murder during the Ziggy-like final concert in Berlin, the Slade character supposedly disappears for ten years, only to resurface as Tommy Stone—a grotesque parody of Bowie during his Serious Moonlight tour of 1983. Slade, it turns out, was born Thomas Brian Stoningham Slade. He has simply taken another variation of his given name and reinvented himself once again; only this time he is linked to right-wing President Reynolds—aka Reagan. Haynes's critique of Bowie provides the impetus for the film's *Citizen Kane*-like structure. The social commentary of the earlier film—the attack on the politics and morals of William Randolph Hearst—is here directed at Bowie's apparent eighties-style sellout to the establishment.

Arthur's life is told in rough parallel to Bowie's career in scenes that are intercut throughout the film. The earliest image we see of Arthur is as a schoolboy drawing a picture of Brian Slade as his English teacher reads from *Dorian Gray*. Likewise, Haynes makes clear that Wilde is the forerunner of glitter music when, himself a schoolboy, Wilde announces, "I want to be a pop idol." However, Haynes makes his clearest connection between Wilde and Slade in a literal media circus in which Slade answers questions from men in suits by quoting Wilde's one-liners. The scene is announced: "The aesthete gives characteristically cynical evidence replete with pointed epigram and startling paradox, while explaining his views on morality in art." While Slade is shown to have mastered Wilde's tactics and techniques, the most heartfelt version of his own ideas is perhaps uttered by a German glitter band that Arthur stumbles onto in Berlin in the film's second half, one of whose members tells him, "We're in a bit of a decadent spiral, aren't we? . . . which is why we prefer impressions to ideas, situations to subjects, brief lights to sustained, exceptions to types." Indeed, the idea that Wilde himself could be an exception, rather than the type of the homosexual that he was to become, is perhaps the film's greatest insight into Wilde's mythos. At the end of the film, Arthur, who has forfeited his own decadent inheritance for a dreary newspaper job, thinks back on an apparently real sexual encounter with Curt Wild, who talked to him about "a freedom. A freedom you can allow yourself. Or not." Arthur has not, of course, allowed himself the freedom from the sexual and gender mores of his society, and he has regretted it. The anarchic freedom of the Wild character is the true freedom of Wilde himself—the refusal to be anything but yourself, a spirit connecting the 1970s with the 1890s. That keeping this connection alive during the fascistic 1980s is difficult is made pointedly clear when Mandy, speaking of Slade's announcement of his bisexuality, says, "Did he realize what he'd actually done? I mean, today, they'd be fighting in the streets. But in 1972, it was more like dancing."

As a young boy who has just witnessed his first same-sex sexual encounter between his vaudevillian aunt, played by Lindsay Kemp in drag, and another man in a backstage room, Slade is inspired to dress up as Little Richard—an early hero of the real Bowie. In addition to the alien genealogy created by the mysterious green stone, we also have another, psychological explanation for the origin of Bowie's desire to dress up, perform, and promote himself. "The music is a mask," says Slade, "while I, in my chiffon and taff, well, varda the message." In *Theatre and Fashion*, the authors note that the first fashion runway was set up in 1900—the year of Wilde's death—when the couturiere Lucile "transformed her new showroom in Hanover Square into a theatre. Building a stage, hanging curtains, and installing crude limelight devices in makeshift wings, she presented London . . . with its first formal fashion show."[56] In a sense, Lucile mirrored—and hence reversed—what Wilde attempted in his social comedies when he turned the stage into a dress shop by emphasizing the characteristics of his characters in the costumes designed for the actors and by extending this commentary to his approach to his own sartorial performance. What happened onstage was ultimately what was copied and worn by the audience themselves. As Frith observes, "Clothes offer the body its most intimate traffic with the outside world."[57] If this is the case, Wilde's performances of self were based not on camp but on economic necessity and a prescient understanding of the market. Haynes also presents Bowie as a master of the market, but one who is willing, like Dorian Gray, to exchange his soul for the illusion of youth in order to continue soullessly in the guise of another body without ever really confronting what he has lost. The film acknowledges this loss for us. The parable of the story, however, seems to be that things lost must be found again. The figure of Wilde returns for each generation in the form in which he is needed most.

Public Encounters with
Private Bodies; or, Rent Music

Bowie's most famous album, *Ziggy Stardust*, presents an elaborate science fiction scenario about the earth's depletion of natural resources and inevitable destruction in five years, the breakdown of the structures of society, the invasion by a group of living black holes who need human bodies to have material form, and the staging of a battle in which Ziggy is literally torn apart at the album's end. Bowie's eccentric and often arcane references in the lyrics to this story are minimal. The album is usually read instead as a parable or allegory about the relationship between a rock and roll singer and his fans. In this sense, Bowie's first major album is similar to the later album *Diamond Dogs* in that it is designed to make his audience self-conscious about the process of their own identification with Bowie himself. The relationship between the performer and the fan is, of necessity, a power dynamic that is almost always sexual in its overtones. In his direct addresses to his fans, Bowie consciously keeps the gender of his fans ambiguous.

In "Music for Pleasure," Simon Frith notes that "for thirty years now British pop iconography, our understanding of what makes music and musicians *sexy*, has depended on a confusion of sexual address. Since David Bowie, such ambiguity has been self-conscious." Indeed, what Frith terms "the rent-boy act" results from the apparently well-known fact that some of the most famous rock managers—Bowie's Ken Pitt or the Beatles' Brian Epstein, for example—were gay.[1] To "pose with the moody innocence of the 1950s" is still a part of what singers do. If this pose is indeed central to the tradition of rock music, it may be because music opens itself up to questions about identity much more readily than other media.[2]

The usual rock star/fan formula in fact assumes a complex connection between the star and his/her audience. Indeed, it is in pop music that we have represented versions of the economic and erotic relationship that Wilde wished to make clear in *De Profundis*. The equation that links desire with spending, for instance, can be found in the music of the Pet Shop Boys in three of their early songs: "Opportunities (Let's Make Lots of Money)," from *Please* (1986), and "Rent" and "Shopping," from *Actually* (1987). Influenced by disco in general and Donna Summer in particular, Neil Tennant and Chris Lowe's music is ideally suited for the intertextual feel of pop music spawned in the postmodern era and the slippage in identity that this implies. "West End Girls," their first hit, was number one on U.S. charts, and though nominally a song about class difference—the "West End girls" contrast with the "East End boys"—the song has been interpreted as one in which "West End girls" is gay slang for male prostitutes.[3] "Opportunities" and "Rent," middling hits in Britain (ranked eleventh and eighth, respectively), are songs about the homoerotics of making and spending together. Although they describe the former as "a joke," Tennant notes that the latter was "performed . . . on the TV variety show, *Live at the Palladium*, with Chris wearing his infamous Issey Miyake blow-up rubber jacket and a painted-on scar." In acknowledging their theatrical edge, the Pet Shop Boys place themselves within a British tradition of gender-bending performances presented on live TV that stretches at least as far back as Roxy Music's performance of "Virginia Plain" on *Top of the Pops*. One of the Pet Shop Boys' more recent albums, *Very* (1993), deals pointedly with gay life as it is lived—whether the fantasy of having tea with Princess Diana that celebrates her impact on gay men during the AIDS crisis, or a remake of the gay pop classic "Go West."

Though the Pet Shop Boys' role in British gay pop music has perhaps been somewhat usurped by the appearance of groups like Blur who appeal to an even younger audience, the Pet Shop Boys have shown the most precise understanding of the underlying connective tissue between Wilde and his various twentieth-century influences. Namely, they play with Wilde's desire to own or control his own identity. Just as Wilde's period at the end of his century provided a fertile ground in which to combine the erotics of identity politics with the economic pleasures of acquisition, the Pet Shop Boys provide a decidedly ironic treatment of the kept gay boy in "Rent." As sung by the boy who is kept, the song is a celebration of the economic and erotic balance the two parties have created and maintained: "You dress me up / I'm your puppet. / You buy me things, / I love it." The song's singular lack of compunction is disarming. "Shopping," which appears just before "Rent," could be a companion piece sung by the same person, though the song is more political in its famous digs at the Tories—"Our gain is your loss / That's the price you pay. / I heard it in the House of Commons / Everything's for sale." A reference to the privatization plan spearheaded by Thatcher and her political cronies, the song's queer subtext of shopping as bonding opens out into a reference to the politics of privilege as exercised in Britain at that time.

"Opportunities," the earliest song, is in fact the most directly Wildean of all the Pet Shop Boys' work: "You've got the brawn / I've got the brains / Let's make lots of money!" Even with its over-the-top musical atmosphere, the song seems in many ways to be the closest to the bone in that it plays with the image that the singers themselves present. Though neither of them can really be thought of as "brains" or "brawn," they do work off this gay stereotype, as other performing duos have, by presenting one quiet musician, Lowe, and one extroverted singer, Tennant. The very nature of the erotics between this seeming pairing of opposites should be clear. It is, however, compounded by various types of role-playing and visual puns on display in later albums. With the two of them often appearing either in matching outfits or in decidedly contrasting ones, their album covers play off the fact that Lowe and Tennant look so much alike. The "clone" aspect of this similarity is referenced in a photo from 1986 that shows Lowe wearing a baseball cap with the word "boy" printed in large letters. Though probably an advertisement for the line of clothing stores by that name, it is also a visual pun on the sort of cross-class attraction that is often played with in their media "look"—one in which Lowe is inevitably photographed as the trade. The crooning Tennant, playing himself, is the one who verbalizes the seduction, even if he is not its author.[4]

The pairings offered by the Pet Shop Boys make clear that the continuum stretching from Wilde's forays with his Bosie into the streets of London continues into the present. The identification with and through the performances offered by Bowie and singers such as the Pet Shop Boys act as only one of the more recent instances of Wilde's influence. That Wilde's own concept of his sexuality is perhaps more clearly a variation on this "new" definition rather than the one developed as "gay" is, I hope, something that I have been able to suggest. Not only is this classification for Wilde an accurate concept to apply to him, but it also applies to many of the changes in cultural production that have overcome music, writing, and performance since the 1980s. That is, the rejection of previous lesbian and gay stereotypes evidenced by Queer Nation, butch/femme, s/m, and other queer centers of activity signals the emergence of a different definition of sexuality alternative to either gay or straight ones that can be seen most readily in popular culture.

In a sense, Pater's preface and conclusion to *The Renaissance* were to his age what Susan Sontag's essay "Against Interpretation" was to hers: a call for a new form of eroticism in criticism with an emphasis on the surface of things and a breaking down of barriers between high and low forms of art to include within the scope of criticism an understanding of the body's relationship to the experience of art. Though hardly new as a concept of aesthetics—a renewal of the senses being one of the oldest definitions—Sontag's attempt to redirect criticism to the focus on the body's reactions to stimuli, most especially to pleasure for its own sake, was a way to bring back Wilde. Not only is her "Notes on 'Camp'" dedicated to him, but as Terry Eagleton understands from the perspective of writing even closer to the millennial edge, Wilde's corporeal aesthetics may well be the only way to make sense of a materialist theory now battered and bruised. With the simultaneous shift from a feminist to a queer studies model in the discourse about gender in the academy, the importance of Wilde is clear: his deconstructive approach to the categorical oppression within bourgeois society was a model for thinking through the problems of capital and gender. Unlike Warhol, Wilde's solution was not to focus solely on the bottom line, profit, in an attempt to make money the ultimate aesthetic valuation, but rather, like Bowie, to create a performative paradigm that was reproducible in and by his disciples and fans that would itself question and complicate, if never overturn, the relationship between style and commerce.

Notes

Introduction

1. Linda Dowling, *Hellenism and Homosexuality in Victorian Oxford* (Ithaca: Cornell University Press, 1994), 119.

2. Jackson notes that the Celtic Revival of the 1890s attempted to combine art with life and was "actually a social movement with a Socialistic tendency." Holbrook Jackson, *The Eighteen Nineties: A Review of Art and Ideas at the Close of the Nineteenth Century* (1913; Harmondsworth, Middlesex: Penguin, 1950), 41.

3. "The faith that others give to what is unseen, I give to what one can touch, and look at." Oscar Wilde, "De Profundis," in *The Soul of Man and Prison Writings*, ed. Isobel Murray (New York: Oxford University Press, 1999), 98.

4. E.g., Lee Edelman, "Homographesis," *Yale Journal of Criticism* 3, no. 1 (1989): 189–207; and Richard Dellamora, *Masculine Desire: The Sexual Politics of Victorian Aestheticism* (Chapel Hill: University of North Carolina Press, 1990).

5. In a recent essay on Schlegel and German romanticism, Nicholas Brown argues that "romanticism is . . . the very ground of post-Romantic thought, even as its later mutations—Modernism and Postmodernism—continue to define themselves against it." Nicholas Brown, "The Eidaesthetic Itinerary: Notes on the Geopolitical Movement of the Literary Absolute," *South Atlantic Quarterly* 100, no. 3 (Summer 2001): 834.

6. Clyde de L. Ryals, *A World of Possibilities: Romantic Irony in Victorian Literature* (Columbus: Ohio State University Press, 1990), 4.

7. Isobel Murray, introduction to *Oscar Wilde*, ed. Isobel Murray (New York: Oxford University Press, 1989), xi.

8. This can probably be seen best in the work of Wilde's French friends. That is, it is fairly easy to see how Verlaine would connect to Mallarmé, who, via symbolism, is but a breath away from Anglo-American modernist writing.

9. The concept of type could be seen as one of many inheritances of Pater. In his essays in *The Renaissance*, Pater developed his own idea of types. As described by Carolyn Williams, "each 'type' represents not only the spirit of its age, but also the consummated achievement of a whole tradition, the summary moment and highest point of a genealogical process." Carolyn Williams, *Transfigured World: Walter Pater's Aesthetic Historicism* (Ithaca: Cornell University Press, 1989), 132.

10. Steven M. L. Aronson, *Hype* (New York: Morrow, 1983).

11. Terry Eagleton, *The Ideology of the Aesthetic* (Cambridge: Basil Blackwell, 1990), 24.

12. By 1832 the term "socialism" was becoming widely used in English and in French. The ideas associated with it were also having influence: the Pre-Raphaelite William Morris ultimately turned away from the brotherhood to pursue socialist aims. Rossetti and Swinburne wrote poetry of topical importance dealing with social reform (and which has to this day remained for the most part unstudied). By the time of *Origin of Species* and *Critique of Political Economy*, 1859, Dickens had already published *Bleak House* (1852) and Flaubert *Madame Bovary* (1856). Scribe's plays were already on the stage, and Lombroso was developing the idea of the criminal type. The influence that socialism and the scientific approach to society had at the height of Victorianism cannot be ignored. Although coming from widely differing political positions, the realistic portrayal of living conditions and social problems united figures such as Flaubert, Marx, and Rossetti and paved the way for the more biological approaches of Zola and the naturalists.

13. Eagleton, *Ideology of the Aesthetic*, 13.

14. Cf. Edouard Roditi: "But in Oscar Wilde's age, the political doctrines of the Dandy and the esthete, who so often professed sympathy with extreme views of the right or the left, were considered dangerous only by the mildly liberal or conservative majority. Had not Lassalle, the German Socialist, been a notorious dandy? Was not Heinrich Heine, esthete and dandy, a close friend of Karl Marx, and had not Wagner at one time been a friend of Bakunin?" Edouard Roditi, *Oscar Wilde* (Norfolk: New Directions, 1947), 148.

15. Terry Eagleton, foreword to *Saint Oscar* (Derry: Field Day, 1989), x.

16. Cf. Jackson: "And it is quite possible that had he lived the even life that he had begun to live on the bleak coast of Normandy after his release from prison, this underlying strain in his character would have turned him into a social reformer. His harrowing letters on prison conditions point to some such destiny, especially" (*The Eighteen Nineties*, 88).

17. Regenia Gagnier, *Idylls of the Marketplace: Oscar Wilde and the Victorian Public* (Stanford: Stanford University Press, 1986), 116; or as Gagnier also observes: "Wilde's radicalism lay in his rendering ironic the commercial image of dandy-artist and his using it dialectically to subvert the image of the bourgeois gentleman, as he did in the debate over *The Picture of Dorian Gray*" (85).

18. Regenia Gagnier, introduction to *Critical Essays on Oscar Wilde*, ed. Regenia Gagnier (New York: G. K. Hall, 1991), 7.

19. Ibid., 7–8; cf. Jackson's version of this line of thought: "Oscar Wilde, for instance, bridged the chasm between the self-contained individualism of the decadents and the communal aspirations of the more advanced social revolutionaries. His essay, *The Soul of Man under Socialism*, has been acclaimed by recognized upholders of Socialism. And even his earlier aestheticism (which belonged to the Eighties) was an attempt to apply the idea of art to mundane affairs" (*The Eighteen Nineties*, 25).

20. Cf. Gagnier: "Elsewhere I have described how for Victorian aesthetes like Ruskin, Morris, and Wilde, aesthetics was conceived broadly, as an art of the everyday rather than the extraordinary." Regenia Gagnier, "On the Instability of Human Wants: Economic and Aesthetic Man," *Victorian Studies* 36, no. 2 (Winter 1993): 149.

21. Indeed, Wilde's materialism is related also to the anarchist communism of Peter Kropotkin—Wilde's "happiest man." Though Kropotkin's emphasis on individualism and the unwavering freedom of individuals within society was to be brought about by people taking back powers now invested with the state, Kropotkin was interested in the ability of the arts to flourish under a new system—one neither communist nor capitalist. Yet the arts were only one of his concerns, and his thinking was definitely non-Epicurean—however significant that "attitude" may be to the history of anarchism. Peter Kropotkin, "Anarchism," in *Kropotkin's Revolutionary Pamphlets*, ed. Roger N. Baldwin (New York: Vanguard Press, 1927), 288. Though Kropotkin does credit "left-wing Hegelians in Germany" with at least temporarily supporting anarchism, his idea of a

full-fledged "individualist anarchism" formed the telos of his thinking. This idea—which he was careful to say was not a model of Utopia—sounded much like the goals in Wilde's *Soul of Man*: "the rehabilitation of the 'I,' the supremacy of the individual, complete 'a-moralism,' and the 'association of the egotists'" (292). Kropotkin listed Carpenter, Whitman, Ibsen, and Zola as important sources "of anarchist ideas [in] modern literature" (299–300): figures extremely important to Wilde's later thought.

22. Oscar Wilde, "The Soul of Man," in *The Soul of Man and Prison Writings*, ed. Isobel Murray (New York: Oxford University Press, 1990), 19.

23. Michel Foucault, *Foucault Live* (New York: Semiotext(e), 1989), 298.

24. Ibid., 311.

25. Ibid., 319.

26. Ibid., 322.

27. Michel Foucault, *The History of Sexuality*, vol. 1, *An Introduction* (New York: Vintage, 1980), 66–67.

28. Ibid., 69.

29. Ibid., 101.

30. Regenia Gagnier, "Production, Reproduction, and Pleasure in Victorian Aesthetics and Economics," in *Victorian Sexual Dissidence*, ed. Richard Dellamora (Chicago: University of Chicago Press, 1999), 135.

31. Ibid., 134.

32. Michael R. Doylen, "Oscar Wilde's *De Profundis*: Homosexual Self-Fashioning on the Other Side of Scandal," *Victorian Literature and Culture* 27, no. 2 (1999): 551.

33. "Yet when Wilde himself imagined his play on stage, he envisioned a synaesthetic picture, appealing to the aural, visual, and olfactory faculties, and emphasizing Salome's effect on the audience. Salome's words were 'like music'; he first wanted her to be costumed in shades of yellow, then in gold or silver, then green like a lizard, then as unadorned as Victorian stages would permit; he wanted braziers of perfume wafting scented clouds before spectacular sets" (Gagnier, *Idylls of the Marketplace*, 165).

1. Wilde's Romantic Irony

1. Eagleton, *Ideology of the Aesthetic*, 174.

2. Cf.: "The essay simply represents an artistic standpoint, and in aesthetic

criticism attitude is everything. . . . It is only in art-criticism, and through it, that we can realize Hegel's system of contraries." Oscar Wilde, "The Truth of Masks," in *The Artist as Critic: Critical Writings of Oscar Wilde*, ed. Richard Ellmann (Chicago: University of Chicago Press, 1969), 432.

3. Peter Allan Dale goes so far as to argue that "what is particularly interesting about Wilde's ongoing preoccupation with crime in the context of Oxford Hegelianism is that it appears to reflect a greater awareness than is found among any of his Oxford contemporaries of the meaning of the dialectic." In fact, after *The Soul of Man* Wilde ceased "to focus on the aesthetic acquisition of harmony between body and soul, which is the goal of the Hegelian Geist and the central preoccupation of such advocates of aesthetic culture as Arnold, Pater, Swinburne and Symonds, [and] he concentrates instead on the process by which humanity moves towards the goal, the dialectical *process*." "Oscar Wilde: Crime and the 'Glorious Shapes of Art,'" *The Victorian Newsletter* 88 (Fall 1995): 4.

4. E.g., "To-day the cry is for Romance." Oscar Wilde, "The Critic as Artist," in *The Artist as Critic: Critical Writings of Oscar Wilde*, ed. Richard Ellmann (Chicago: University of Chicago Press, 1969), 390.

5. For example, to Wilde the Middle Ages often represent a superior time to his own because of the association of artificial, antimimetic design—the obverse of realism. Yet Wilde uses the term "Renaissance" in a somewhat ahistorical way to discuss the period since the French Revolution—that is, since the current "crisis of representation," as Seyhan terms it, began. Azade Seyhan, *Representation and Its Discontents: The Critical Legacy of German Romanticism* (Berkeley: University of California Press, 1992), 5. Likewise, "Hellenic" is usually meant to refer to a debased form of Athenian culture, but for Wilde it signifies a return to things Greek in his own day. Wilde's various senses of historical terminology—like all of his uses of important recurring terms—are often confusing and too few for the many distinctions he tries to make at different times.

6. Pater likewise uses the terms in seemingly confusing ways, as when he writes: "The writings of the 'romantic school,' of which the aesthetic poetry is an afterthought, mark a transition not so much from the pagan to the mediaeval ideal, as from a lower to a higher degree of passion in literature. The end of the eighteenth century, swept by vast disturbing currents, experienced an excitement of spirit of which one note was a reaction against an outworn classicism

severed not more from nature than from the genuine motives of ancient art; and a return to true Hellenism was as much a part of this reaction as the sudden pre-occupation with things mediaeval." Walter Pater, *Sketches and Reviews* (New York: Boni and Liveright, 1919), 2.

7. Oscar Wilde, "Mr. Pater's Last Volume," in *The Artist as Critic: Critical Writings of Oscar Wilde*, ed. Richard Ellmann (Chicago: University of Chicago Press, 1969), 230.

8. Marjorie Levinson theorizes that "the postmodern" might be thought as "what arises from the death of dialectics, is itself a dialectical phenomenon: the afterlife of dialectics. As such it is both conservative and liberatory, static and dynamic, culturally absorptive and impermeable, not because it is in some abstruse way 'undecidable' but because it is bound up with the history and logic of capital and, like all such developments, it is deeply subversive in its effects." Marjorie Levinson, "Romantic Poetry: The State of the Art," *Modern Language Quarterly* 54, no. 2 (June 1993): 198.

9. Walter Pater, *Appreciations* (Evanston: Northwestern University Press, 1987), 243.

10. Ibid., 243–44.

11. Ibid., 256.

12. Cf. Chamberlin: "The self-idolatry of Baudelaire's dandy is basically the refined egotism of romantic poetics, without which the artist can accomplish neither self-discovery nor self-destruction." J. E. Chamberlin, *Ripe Was the Drowsy Hour: The Age of Oscar Wilde* (London: Seabury, 1977), 86.

13. Although I will only discuss the work of the Schlegels and Novalis (Friedrich von Hardenberg) in any detail, I do want to note that many other figures are related to this movement in various ways: Achim von Arnim, Clemens Brentano, Joseph von Eichendorff, E. T. A. Hoffmann, Friedrich Hölderlin, Jean Paul Richter, and Ludwig Tieck, not to mention Friedrich Wilhelm von Schelling, Friedrich von Schiller, and Friedrich Schleiermacher. Kant and Hegel are also important as an influence and a parallel development, respectively. For a general history of the movement—and its differences from other forms of Anglo-Continental romanticism—see Ernst Behler, *German Romantic Literary Theory* (Cambridge: Cambridge University Press, 1993).

14. Eric A. Blackall, *The Novels of the German Romantics* (Ithaca: Cornell University Press, 1983), 20.

15. Julia Prewitt Brown, *Cosmopolitan Criticism: Oscar Wilde's Philosophy of Art* (Charlottesville: University Press of Virginia, 1997), 62.

16. The type of irony that Schlegel first outlined was termed "artistic irony" by Kierkegaard and, by Schlegel, "irony of irony" or "poetry of poetry." The phrase "romantic irony," as Lilian Furst has shown, came later. Lilian R. Furst, *Fictions of Romantic Irony* (Cambridge: Harvard University Press, 1984), 29–30.

17. Wilde also makes this point in several places, but perhaps most emphatically in "The Critic as Artist," when he has Gilbert say: "Yes, Ernest: the contemplative life, the life that has for its aim not *doing* but *being*, and not *being* merely, but *becoming*—that is what the critical spirit gave us" (384).

18. Albert Guérard, *Art for Art's Sake* (New York: Lothrop, Lee and Shepard, 1936), 37. Guérard recognized a connection as early as 1936: "But we should be courting disappointment if we expected too neat a coincidence between Romanticism and Art for Art's Sake. If Art for Art's Sake is an elusive formula, Romanticism is even more Protean. Both are not so much doctrines as attitudes—and we are not excluding the least favorable interpretation of the word *attitude*, namely a *pose*" (35).

19. Mario Praz, *The Romantic Agony*, trans. Angus Davidson (1933; New York: World Publishing, 1968), 289.

20. As Julia Prewitt Brown notes, "in *The Picture of Dorian Gray* the romantic idea of criticism is at last fulfilled: a work of criticism become an autonomous work of art, as Friedrich Schlegel had demanded it should be, and as Wilde had wanted to be in both 'The Decay of Lying' and 'The Portrait of Mr. W. H.'" (*Cosmopolitan Criticism*, 77). Benjamin, as she notes, would continue the enfolding of the critical with the creative into the next century (73).

21. Eagleton, *Ideology of the Aesthetic*, 174.

22. Ibid., 175.

23. Ibid., 176.

24. For Gautier, however, the use of dialogue standing alone is at least part of the antiromanticist doctrine of the Parnassian school that he promotes in the famous preface added to the novel. He saw the artistic practice of this school as objective; hence he believed that it was important for the reader not to confuse the author of the novel with the characters, who should speak for themselves. Jessica R. Feldman, *Gender on the Divide: The Dandy in Modernist Literature* (Ithaca: Cornell University Press, 1989), 52. It is more difficult to know what

Swinburne had in mind, as his novel is unfinished, though his posthumous notes seem to show that he was experimenting along the same lines as Schlegel. In that case, the fact that both *Lesbia Brandon* and *Lucinde* were left unfinished may indicate in part a tacit belief that the project of romanticism can never conclude.

25. The fusing of criticism with fiction, as in *Lucinde* and *Dorian Gray*, had already been explored in Novalis's *Heinrich von Ofterdingen* (1799–1800) to an even fuller extent. Seyhan describes it as "a configuration of various literary forms which narrate the story of their own historical and formal production. The conceptual tapestry of the novel, where various reflections on the nature of understanding, interpretation, and knowledge are interwoven, makes a ready categorization of the work untenable" (*Representation and Its Discontents*, 116).

26. Wilde's best description of his view of the Socratic dialogue can be found in "The Critic as Artist": "Dialogue, certainly, that wonderfully literary form which, from Plato to Lucian, and from Lucian to Giordano Bruno, and from Bruno to that grand old Pagan in whom Carlyle took such delight, the creative critics of the world have always employed, can never lose for the thinker its attraction as a mode of expression. By its means he can both reveal and conceal himself, and give form to every fancy, and reality to every mood. But it means he can exhibit the object from each point of view, and show it to us in the round, as a sculptor shows us things, gaining in this manner all the richness and reality of effect that comes from those side issues that are suddenly suggested by the central idea in its progress, and really illumine the idea more completely, or from those felicitous after-thoughts that give a fuller completeness to the central scheme, and yet convey something of the delicate charm of chance" (391).

27. Patricia Flanagan Behrendt, *Oscar Wilde: Eros and Aesthetics* (New York: St. Martin's, 1991), 109.

28. The relationship between the Socratic dialogue, the dramatic monologue, and drama is a complex one that can only be touched on here. In Wilde's case, I agree with Small that "Wilde wished [in *Intentions*] . . . to locate his views away from the more usual vehicle for criticism in the 1890s, the periodical or scholarly essay. A clear implication from this decision about genre is that Wilde was anticipating from his contemporary readers a set of responses quite different from those elicited by the writer of the periodical essay. By employing techniques derived from some kinds of drama, Wilde seems to have wanted to produce an argument dependent upon dialectic: to use, that is, one of the

specific devices of philosophical dialogue. By the 1890s . . . one of the most usual academic ways of discussing the genre of philosophical dialogue, and in particular the *Dialogues* of Plato, was to stress the effect of the dramatic elements of the texts in question—to see in the speakers in a philosophical dialogue something akin to dramatic characterization. In this view, philosophical argument is not stated: rather, being provisional and unsystematic, it emerges in the course of the dialogue." Ian Small, *Conditions for Criticism: Authority, Knowledge, and Literature in the Late Nineteenth Century* (Oxford: Clarendon, 1991), 120. Small also notes that cheap editions of Plato were plentiful at the time Wilde was writing his dialogues (109), and that though most reviewers of *Intentions* thought the dialogues were not serious enough, they missed the point in that they play with tweaking "critical authority" (121).

29. Behrendt, *Oscar Wilde*, 109.

30. Friedrich Schlegel, *Friedrich Schlegel's "Lucinde" and the "Fragments"* (Minneapolis: University of Minnesota Press, 1971), 189.

31. Ryals, *A World of Possibilities*, 6.

32. As Blackall describes it, "progressive universal poetry" is an attempt to "combine poetry and prose, enthusiasm and critical stance, and maintain a free equipoise between what is represented and the representing agent." This type of poetry "is not established as a given, but is and will always be in process of developing itself" (22).

33. Ryals, *A World of Possibilities*, 7. As he goes on to say, the artist, "both *in* and *out* of the creation. . . . Hovering above his work but free to enter it as he pleases, the artist is like . . . the Harlequin figure . . . who at the same time controls the plot and mocks the play" (7).

34. In a particularly Schlegelian moment in his Oxford notebook, Wilde seems to understand this definition of poetry: "Philosophy passes into mysticism because it cannot answer its own questions: the highest truth of philosophy is rational and self-conscious poetry: and the highest poetry is often irrational and unconscious philosophy." Philip E. Smith II and Michael S. Helfand, eds., *Oscar Wilde's Oxford Notebooks: A Portrait of Mind in the Making* (New York: Oxford University Press, 1989), 144.

35. Friedrich Schlegel, *Dialogue on Poetry and Literary Aphorisms*, trans. Ernst Behler and Roman Struc (University Park: Pennsylvania State University Press, 1968), 83.

36. Seyhan, *Representation and Its Discontents*, 19.

37. Schlegel, *Lucinde*, 145.

38. In "The English Renaissance," Wilde says, "Nor is it again that the novel has killed the play, as some critics would persuade us—the romantic movement of France shows us that. The work of Balzac and of Hugo grew up side by side together; nay, more, were complementary to each other, though neither of them saw it." Oscar Wilde, "The English Renaissance of Art," in *Miscellanies*, ed. Robert Ross (London: Dawsons of Pall Mall, 1969), 264.

39. Stanley Weintraub, "Disraeli and Wilde's *Dorian Gray*," *Unisa English Studies* 31, no. 2 (1993): 32. Indeed, Weintraub says that Wilde's description of Meredith is better saved for *Vivian Grey*: "It is a remarkable though very unequal performance, full of insolence and naiveté, with excellent thumb-nail sketches of character and a heap of epigrams lost in a frantic purposeless plot and floods of would-be German romanticism" (29).

40. In their introduction to Wilde's notebooks, Smith and Helfand create an alternate narrative for the philosophical and critical influences at work in Wilde's writing and thinking as evidenced, mainly, by the schools of thought he was exposed to while in college. They seek to expand the relatively narrow range of thought that Wilde is usually put into (as a minor figure feeding off the work of Arnold and Pater, for instance). As they say, most critics "have limited their attention to literary and artistic traditions such as aestheticism, symbolism, and decadence, and so have exaggerated the importance of one strand in the complex fabric of Wilde's critical position. In their search for a usable literary past, they have defined Wilde as an art-for-art's-sake critic who is a precursor of modern critical theory and a major bridge from Victorian aestheticism to modern aesthetics. Here we argue that Wilde's critical position properly belongs not to the art-for-art's-sake movement but to the traditions of late Victorian cultural criticism" (42). German romanticism is one of the many influences that they attempt to link Wilde to via a structural connection in his thinking: "The attraction of analogy, which Wilde uses to link science with other forms of thought, has at its root the idealists' belief in the fundamentally harmonious structure and development of reality. Like the English and German Romantics, Wilde sees the imagination, the analogizing power, as the fundamental quality of mind. This critical-creative union informs the theory and structure of Wilde's later work and explains his attempts to develop dialectically such forms as dialogues,

fictionalized biographical and critical studies, the novel of ideas, and even aphorisms. A title such as 'The Critic as Artist' reveals his assumption of this relationship and its continuity in his critical thought. In that essay he insists on the
necessity of the critical faculty for the creative writer and of the creative aspect
of critical writing. Wilde sees criticism as serving an essentially antagonistic or
antithetical intellectual and social function. The spirit is realized in and through
opposition to custom, habit, and stasis. Wilde adopted an appropriate rhetorical stance which characterizes his later work, namely, taking elements of mid-
Victorian political, philosophical, and scientific beliefs and developing their
subversive implications" (38).

41. Guérard notes that the Continental writers "were satiric with a reassur-
ing wink. . . . [But it] was from Byron . . . that they borrowed their dominant
mood, the flippant dandical tone of *Don Juan*," for in fact "self-irony is a natural
development for those in whom Romantic frenzy is imitative" (47).

42. Blackall, *Novels*, 23–24.

43. Cf. Small: "And it is precisely this fundamental revaluation of the relationship between art and life which is the key concern of all Aesthetic criticism
and which allows the modern reader a way of exploring the revolutionary nature
of the movement." Ian Small, ed., *The Aesthetes: A Sourcebook* (Boston: Routledge,
1979), xii.

44. Anne K. Mellor, *English Romantic Irony* (Cambridge: Harvard University
Press, 1980), 19–20.

45. The criticism to which Symons is referring is the type that Pater collects
in *Essays and Studies*, such as "Notes on Some Pictures of 1868," in which he
writes: "His [Albert Moore's] painting is to artists what the verse of Thèophile
Gautier is to poets; the faultless and secure expression of an exclusive worship
of things formally beautiful" (360). Interestingly, Huysmans wrote two books of
art criticism: *L'Art Moderne* and *Certains*.

46. Cf. Praz: "Moreau composed his pictures in the style of symphonic
poems, loading them with significant accessories in which the principal theme
was echoed, until the subject yielded the last drop of its symbolic sap" (290).

47. Roditi, *Oscar Wilde*, 22.

48. For other examples in Wilde, Roditi notes that "Wilde thus called his
critical essay on Thomas Griffiths Wainewright a 'study in green,' described
some of Dvořák's music as 'curiously colored' or a 'mad scarlet thing,' and wrote

The Birthday of the Infanta, one of his fairy-tales, after the manner of Velázquez, though he never stated it, much as Hoffmann had once written *Princess Brambilla* 'after the manner of Jacques Callot' or as the poet Aloysius Bertrand had composed the prose poems of *Gaspard de la Nuit* after the manner of the same fantastic draftsman" (23).

49. Chamberlin, *Ripe Was the Drowsy Hour*, 43.

50. Ibid., 70.

51. Oscar Wilde, *The Picture of Dorian Gray*, ed. Peter Ackroyd (New York: Penguin, 1985), 23.

52. As Furst notes, the importance of the visual, the image, has parallels with irony: "The transferal of irony from the verbal to the metaphysical domain entailed a change in its literary character too. Like the image, which underwent a parallel metamorphosis at about the same time under the impact of the same cultural constellation, irony rose from the position of servant to that of master" (*Fictions of Romantic Irony*, 36).

53. "The Disciple," a retelling of the Narcissus myth, is perhaps the most important precursor to the prose poetry of *Dorian Gray*.

54. "Of all the forms of literature that of the prose poem was Des Esseintes' chosen favourite. Handled by an alchemist of genius, it should, according to him, store up in its small compass, like an extract of meat, so to say, the essence of the novel, while suppressing its long, tedious analytical passages and superfluous descriptions. Again and again Des Esseintes had pondered the distracting problem, how to write a novel concentrated in a few sentences, but which should yet contain the cohabited juice of the hundreds of pages always taken up in describing the setting, sketching the characters, gathering together the necessary incidental observations and minor details. In that case, so inevitable and unalterable would be the words selected that they must take the place of all others; in so ingenious and masterly a fashion would each adjective be chosen that it could not with any justice be robbed of its right to be there, and would open up such wide perspectives as would set the reader dreaming for weeks together of its meaning, at once precise and manifold." J. K. Huysmans, *Against the Grain*, with an introduction by Havelock Ellis (New York: Three Sirens, 1931), 311.

55. Ibid., 310.

56. It should perhaps be noted here the importance of sound to the poetry of not only Tennyson and Swinburne but also Verlaine and Mallarmé. Both melodic

and visual, the poetic style of the slick surface was quite possibly copied by Wilde in the passages discussed here.

57. Oscar Wilde, "Pen, Pencil, and Poison," in *The Artist as Critic: Critical Writings of Oscar Wilde*, ed. Richard Ellmann (Chicago: University of Chicago Press, 1969), 330.

58. Isobel Armstrong, *Victorian Poetry: Poetry, Poetics, and Politics* (New York: Routledge, 1993), 405.

59. Ibid., 417.

60. Ibid., 418.

61. Ryals, *A World of Possibilities*, 12.

62. Ibid., 13.

63. Gagnier, *Idylls of the Marketplace*, 33.

64. Furst, *Fictions of Romantic Irony*, 230.

65. Wilde, "The Critic as Artist," 389.

66. Oscar Wilde, "The Truth of Masks," in *The Artist as Critic: Critical Writings of Oscar Wilde*, ed. Richard Ellmann (Chicago: University of Chicago Press, 1969), 432.

67. In his autobiography, Yeats quotes Wilde on this subject: "'Olive Schreiner,' he said once to me, 'is staying in the East End because that is the only place where people do not wear masks upon their faces, but I have told her that I live in the West End because nothing in life interests me but the mask.'" Yeats, *The Autobiography of William Butler Yeats* (1916; New York: Collier, 1965). Indeed, the mask becomes an extremely important motif for Yeats himself and shows up in *A Vision* as important to "Phase 19," whose "Examples" include Wilde, Byron, and D'Annunzio, who represent a type: "The strength from conviction, derived from a *Mask* of the first quarter *antithetically* transformed, is not founded upon social duty, though that may seem so to others, but is temperamentally formed to fit some crisis of personal life." Yeats, *A Vision* (1937; New York: Collier, 1967), 148.

68. See Clyde de L. Ryals, *From the Great Deep: Essays on "Idylls of the King"* (Columbus: Ohio State University Press, 1967).

69. Carol T. Christ, *Victorian and Modern Poetics* (Chicago: Universtiy of Chicago Press, 1984), 32.

70. Wilde, *The Picture of Dorian Gray*, 194.

71. Ibid., 66.

72. Ibid., 70.

73. Andrew Elfenbein, "Byronism and the Work of Homosexual Performance in Early Victorian England," *Modern Language Quarterly* 54, no. 4 (December 1993): 552–53.

2. Attributing Wilde

1. Although, admittedly, much of the play would have been unaffected—and some of the dialogue and innuendos in the original version are more explicitly queer—the play did improve with the cuts and alterations. For a discussion of the differences some of these changes made, see Eve Kosofsky Sedgwick, "Tales of the Avunculate: Queer Tutelage in *The Importance of Being Earnest*," in *Tendencies* (Durham: Duke University Press, 1993).

2. Richard Ellmann, *Oscar Wilde* (New York: Knopf, 1988), 540.

3. As Nunokawa and others make clear, Wilde's sexuality until his post-prison years may have been an ambiguous and complicated one. In part, his turning toward men as his main sexual enjoyment may have had to do with his feeling less desire for his wife, Constance Lloyd, after her pregnancies. Of course, it may also be that Wilde's sexuality either changed or that he became bolder about indulging his desires for men and boys. In either case, the ambiguity of *Dorian Gray* may be explained by Wilde's own inability either to admit same-sex attraction to himself as his primary sexual desire or even to decide what he mainly thought about it. Instead of instituting same-sex desire as primary, *Dorian Gray* raises it as a question but refuses to give the reader a definite answer. Nunokawa notes that "this narrative is the most recent and most liberal administration of a denominational regime first instated by the entomological zeal of nineteenth century sexology, and later crystallized in twentieth century psychoanalysis and psychotherapy; a regime which lodges desire and identity in a tautological relation; a regime that defines who I am as what I want." Jeff Nunokawa, "Homosexual Desire and the Effacement of the Self in *The Picture of Dorian Gray*," *American Imago* 49, no. 3 (1992): 313. In another context, Ellis Hanson makes a similar argument: "She [Eve Kosofsky Sedgwick] sees the tension between the figural and the structural in *Dorian Gray* as an essentially modernist and homophobic strategy of abstract formalism, by which the literary frame is emptied of specific homosexual content. I would argue rather that this tension between the figural and the structural might indicate an essentially

postmodernist—or at any rate, decadent—gesture on Wilde's part by which he unmasks the real as a fiction, another mask, essentially textual. In other words, sin is not an act so much as an interpretation. It is an act determined by the practice of interpretation. In this way, the sin is not in the transgression, but in the confession that produces the transgression as such. For Wilde, the confession determines the sin, rather than the sin the confession. Dorian's murder of Basil is certainly a relatively direct representation of a transgressive act, but there are other sins in the novel that seem to be the mere conversational traces of a transgression that is otherwise unrepresented. We get only a confession, a look of shame, a recollection of pleasure. We see the confessional closet, and it might be an empty closet, but that is all we require." Ellis Hanson, *Decadence and Catholicism* (Cambridge: Harvard University Press, 1997), 288.

4. Composed of tales, *Melmoth* has the same romance structure as Byron's *Childe Harold*, and the book's protagonist is always reading older works. As Praz notes, "The central episode of the novel (which is made up of several stories one inside the other, like the *Thousand and One Nights* . . . which Maturin quotes) consists of the love-affair of Melmoth, who here conforms to the type of the enamoured fiend in Oriental tales." Mario Praz, *The Romantic Agony*, trans. Angus Davidson (1933; New York: World Publishing, 1968), 218. The book also contains a version of sadism that was admired by Baudelaire.

5. Wayne Koestenbaum, "Wilde's Hard Labor and the Birth of Gay Reading," in *Engendering Men*, ed. Joseph Boone and Michael Cadden (New York: Routledge, 1990), 177.

6. I would like for my discussion of "type" not only to reference Koestenbaum's meanings in his essay but also to resonate with Armstrong's use of the term in "Introduction: Rereading Victorian Poetry," in her *Victorian Poetry* (1993). Drawing on Carlyle's *Sartor Resartus* (1831), Armstrong plays with his idea of "movable types" to suggest that "'type' is movable because printing removes language and places it and its effects beyond the control of the writer. It is subject to arbitrary interpretation and because of this the fixed and universal 'Type,' ultimately a theological notion, embodying permanent values, can no longer sustain itself and is the subject of arbitrary signification. Money works in the same way and the currency of money and print are connected." Isobel Armstrong, *Victorian Poetry: Poetry, Poetics, and Politics* (New York: Routledge, 1993), 5. Armstrong ultimately teases out some of the connections between the

instability of the relationship between language and its control by the writer and what this might suggest for deconstructive readings of the literature of the period—especially as has to do with the contradictions of the "double poem" and the necessity of an "active reader."

7. Koestenbaum, "Wilde's Hard Labor," 181.

8. Neil Bartlett, *Who Was That Man? A Present for Mr. Oscar Wilde* (London: Serpent's Tail, 1988), 63.

9. Alan Sinfield, *The Wilde Century: Effeminacy, Oscar Wilde, and the Queer Moment* (New York: Columbia University Press, 1994), 125.

10. Ibid., 38.

11. Of course, this entire realm of speculation is complicated by the fact that in naming homosexuality—or homosexual desire—it would have been difficult to know what was being named at that time (or now, for that matter). Certainly, as we know that Wilde did not enjoy anal sex, "sodomite" was technically wrong. Likewise, the very resistance to naming the desire directly—as was clear at the time—may have been part of a truthful realization that naming it was simply bewildering, especially if one considers the various disjunctions between doing something and thinking about doing something, having done something and not planning to do it again, et cetera. For more on this, see "Axiomatic," in Eve Kosofsky Sedgwick's *Epistemology of the Closet* (Berkeley: University of California Press, 1990).

12. Indeed, *De Profundis* is never really Wilde's own in that it was never published during his lifetime. The only volume of Wilde's complete works ever assembled—the 1908 edition by Ross—contains only an expurgated edition of it. Not until 1962 was a complete text published in book form. Even then, Wilde's own title was not included. The rather moralistic and generic title of *De Profundis*, with its hint of contrition, was used by Ross—apparently to garner sympathy. Wilde's title, by contrast, not only contains more of a political cast but is also rather erotic. As in Swinburne's "Fragoletta," Wilde's letter to his lover—to the love of his life—depicts him speaking to the one loved while "in prison and in chains." Wilde emphasizes his body, his discomfort, and his specific subject position as one who is very much in bondage and is writing a love letter in that state.

13. Bartlett, *Who Was That Man*, 209.

14. As Small notes, "Little is known . . . of the collaborative nature of Wilde's

work, although there is abundant evidence that he *must* have collaborated in large measure with George Alexander and Herbert Beerbohm Tree." Ian Small, *Oscar Wilde Revalued: An Essay on New Methods and Methods of Research* (Greensboro: ELT, 1993), 8.

15. "Nouvelles nouvelles" could be translated as "new tales" or "new stories," or, with a contemporary twist, "short stories." The title given to the first tale is sometimes "The Reverse of the Medal," but it has also been translated simply as "The Reverse Side." The point, of course, is that the topic of the story is the backside. This image is explored in several of the tales scattered throughout the book. I would like to thank Diane Sepanski for discovering the connection between the subtitle and the French romance—and for bringing it to my attention.

16. Oscar Wilde, *The Picture of Dorian Gray*, ed. Peter Ackroyd (New York: Penguin, 1985), 69.

17. Ibid., 156.

18. Ibid., 140.

19. Ibid., 155.

20. Robert B. Douglas, introduction to *The Hundred Stories*, trans. Robert B. Douglas (New York: Ace Books, n.d.), 18.

21. In his contemporary translation of *Les Cent Nouvelles*, Russell Hope Robbins criticizes Douglas's translation as being of "little value: it is based not on the manuscript but on the inferior printed text, is cut almost a quarter of the original length, and is full of serious errors in translation" (v). While some of this is no doubt true, it is also important to keep in mind that Douglas's translation is more contemporary to *Teleny*, as Robbins claims that it was "produced" in 1889, which would make its publication predate *Teleny*'s writing by one year. Likewise, the later attribution of the whole text to Vigneulles is a theory that was not available at the end of the nineteenth century, when the general belief was that *The Hundred Stories* was coordinated and edited by a learned person of some type but was written and partially edited by several men. If one examines the editions of the book published in the nineteenth century—the 1863 edition by Garnier Frères Libraires-Éditeurs or the 1874 edition by Édition Jouaust—one can see that the theory put forth by Douglas is the one that seems to have been accepted by the editors and publishers of the time, and, indeed, well into the twentieth century. What is more convincing is Robbins's noting that "the

logical setting is Duke Philip's court" rather than the castle at which Louis bided his time before returning home. Russell Hope Robbins, introduction to *The Hundred Tales* [*Les Cent Nouvelles Nouvelles*], trans. Russell Hope Robbins (New York: Crown, 1960), xii.

22. As with *Les Cent Nouvelles*, we may never know how much of *Teleny* was composed by the mysterious editor. In *Les Cent Nouvelles*, "The Reverse of the Medal" and other stories are attributed to Monseigneur Le Duc. That this means Duke Philippe seems obvious, though it may refer to Louis, or, again, to someone else altogether. Antoine de La Salle appears as an author under his own name, yet there is also an anonymous author who goes by the simple title "L'Acteur" (Editor). If he is the editor, then why is there a separate "Le Duc," whose identity is unknown? Who was that (noble)man?

23. Quoted in Winston Leyland, introduction to *Teleny*, ed. Winston Leyland (San Francisco: Gay Sunshine, 1984), 5.

24. Ibid., 6.

25. Ibid.

26. Ibid., 7.

27. Brake argues that even books about nineteenth-century pornography such as Steven Marcus's *The Other Victorians* "themselves became part of coterie reading . . . outside of the mainstream of criticism and the dominant interpretative community." Laurel Brake, *Subjugated Knowledges: Journalism, Gender, and Literature in the Nineteenth Century* (New York: New York University Press, 1994), 127.

28. Leyland, introduction to *Teleny*, 7–8.

29. Ibid., 8.

30. Ibid., 9.

31. What is perhaps more truly puzzling is that the French edition—the original edition—is actually shorter than the first English translation. That is, though the first edition is obviously based on the one seen by Hirsch, someone must have added material before it was printed. Leyland argues that it was Smithers who made the changes.

32. As Kate Chedgzoy argues in a discussion of Shakespeare's *Sonnets* in "The Portrait of Mr. W. H.," "in misrepresenting the historical contexts of patronage and manuscript circulation in which the *Sonnets* were originally produced. . . . [t]he *Sonnets* are reconstructed in the image of the homosexual coterie publications with which Wilde himself was involved—magazines such as *The Spirit Lamp*

and *The Chameleon*, and the collectively written work of homosexual pornography, *Teleny*." Kate Chedgzoy, *Shakespeare's Queer Children: Sexual Politics and Contemporary Culture* (New York: Manchester University Press, 1995), 144.

33. Oscar Wilde [attributed], *Teleny*, ed. Winston Leyland (San Francisco: Gay Sunshine, 1984), 23.

34. Ibid., 28.

35. Ibid., 26.

36. Ibid., 31.

37. Ibid., 32.

38. "The Reverse of the Medal," in *The Hundred Stories*, trans. Robert B. Douglas (New York: Ace Books, n.d.), 23.

39. Peter Wagner notes that in eighteenth-century France Crébillon *fils* "usher[ed] in [a] wave of licentious 'oriental' narratives; but it is obvious that he borrowed from Galland's translation of the *Arabian Nights*, as well as from the French *fabliaux*." Peter Wagner, *Eros Revived: Erotica of the Enlightenment in England and America* (London: Secker and Warburg, 1988), 206. Both genres, in other words, were known to be originary sources for erotica—as were Greek dialogues before and after them.

40. The erotic economy of *The Hundred Stories* is probably of a depth I can only begin to touch on here. Indeed, much of what is going on in representing backsides may well have to do with subversion—whether truly radical or of a type that would ultimately support the status quo—and with sexual and scatological jokes. For instance, is the woman performing fellatio on the neighbor when the husband comes in? Is the reduction of women to so much "tail" an attempt to commodify them—or even to suggest their power within society?

41. *Urning*, perhaps the most common name for what would become "homosexual," comes from *Uranos*, which means "heaven": a love above the ordinary, à la the *Symposium*, which Ulrichs invents from the Greek. Of course, "Ernest" (or one who is "Earnest") is a probable pun.

42. "The Priest and the Acolyte," *Chameleon* 1, no. 1 (December 1894).

43. Wilde has been linked to translations of other works as well—such as Ibsen's *When We Dead Awaken*, which was actually translated into English by William Archer in 1900. Though Wilde attempted to use translation as a way to make money on the side during the relatively lean first few years of marriage, much of this translation was probably published anonymously—if at all. Though in 1888 Wilde talked of a planned translation of Flaubert's "Tentation,"

Flaubert's most Oriental piece of writing, it will always be difficult to identify which translations Wilde did and did not do. It is extremely important, however, to note the extent to which his name was attached to various projects as a way to suggest a queer association. In other words, his name's ability to do the work of selling—even if posthumously or not to his knowledge—was certainly used in the semiprivacy of the world of private printing and, more than likely, in the hypercapitalistic realm of the pornography market of his day, and perhaps especially during the period of modernism that followed his death. See Rod Boroughs, "Oscar Wilde's Translation of Petronius: The Story of a Literary Hoax," *English Language in Transition, 1880–1920* 38, no. 1 (1995): 8–49.

44. Cf. Roditi: "Later, in the piled-up Oriental imagery of *The Fisherman and His Soul* and *The Star Child*, born of eighteenth-century translations and imitations of *The Arabian Nights*, improved in the Regency schools of Beckford's *Vathek*, Morier's *Haiji Baba*, Moore's *Lalla Rookh* or the architectural fantasies of the Brighton Pavilion, then perfected by French Romantic art in the odalisques of Ingres and Delacroix till the Orient almost ceased to be exotic in Fitzgerald's *Omar Khayyam*, in the art of Fromentin and in the poetry of Leconte de Lille, we discover Wilde's attempt, through the use of vivid and surprising detail, to maintain the barbaric and exotic values of Orientalism, much as St.-J. Perse has done in twentieth-century poetry: 'From the roof of a house a company of women watched us. One of them wore a mask of gilded leather.'" Edouard Roditi, *Oscar Wilde* (Norfolk: New Directions, 1947), 24.

45. Roditi argues that opium came to Wilde from the German romantics via Novalis and Schelling, who had passed it on to Baudelaire and De Quincey, among others.

46. Powell notes that there was a play by Sidney Grundy, *The Arabian Nights: A Farcical Comedy in Three Acts* (1887)—performed in 1892 and 1896—that may have suggested the idea of Bunberrying: "The hero . . . desperate to evade his tyrannical mother-in-law, disguises himself as Caliph Haroun al Raschid and goes about London doing good deeds and ingratiating himself with pretty girls. The idea came to him when—'in order to escape that eye' of his wife's mother—he shut himself in his bedroom with a volume of *The Arabian Nights*. 'My imagination was fired,' explains Arthur Hummingtop. 'I felt myself every inch a caliph. In my excitement, I disguised myself.'" Kerry Powell, *Oscar Wilde and the Theatre of the 1890s* (New York: Cambridge University Press, 1990), 128.

47. As Marcel Hénaff notes, "It is obvious that the dominant paradigm in Sade is a world where machines begin to impose themselves and where mechanical functioning is grasped and reformulated as a way of desubjectivizing bodies, as the affirmation and production of the pleasure of quantities." Marcel Hénaff, "Sade, the Mechanization of the Libertine Body, and the Crisis of Reason," trans. Anne-Marie Feenberg, in *Technology and the Politics of Knowledge*, ed. Andrew Feenberg and Alastair Hannay (Bloomington: Indiana University Press, 1995), 227.

48. Cf. Schlegel's remarks in his "Dialogue on Poetry": "In the same way Boccaccio's mind established for the poets of every nation an inexhaustible source of peculiar, mostly true, and very thoroughly elaborated stories, which through their power of expression and the excellent structure of his periods raised the narrative language of conversation to a solid foundation for the prose of the novel." Friedrich Schlegel, *Dialogue on Poetry and Literary Aphorisms*, with an introduction by Ernst Behler and Roman Struc (University Park: Pennsylvania State University Press, 1968), 68.

49. Sade's *La philosophie dans le boudoir* is especially important here in that its main theme is the joys of anal sex—for both "straight" and "gay" partners. Like the novels of the German romantics, it is written almost like a play, with dialogue markers and even parenthetical "stage directions" throughout. The pedagogical function and its relationship to sex and knowledge is made explicit in a translation of one particular description of action: "To show Eugénie how 'tis to be done, he socratizes Augustin himself." Sade's polemic, that the anus was made to be fucked, is an argument amply made by the book. Donatien Alphonse François de Sade, *The Bedroom Philosophers*, trans. Pieralessandro Casavini (Paris: Olympia, 1965), 102.

50. Crompton writes that "Byron would surely have relished anticipating Burton" (127). As he notes earlier: "When Byron first read *Vathek, an Arabian Tale*, is unknown; it was first published in 1786. But Beckford's fantastic romance, purportedly the history of Haroun-al-Raschid's grandson, fascinated him for a variety of reasons, not the least of which must have been its bisexual ambience." Louis Crompton, *Byron and Greek Love: Homophobia in 19th-Century England* (Berkeley: University of California Press, 1985), 118.

51. Symonds's book was the first serious work on homosexuality published in the United Kingdom. Though Symonds disliked the "morbid and Perfumed"

Dorian Gray and advocated what he considered the more Whitmanesque "athletic" or "manly" versions of male-male love, his essay was made a part of Havelock Ellis's *Sexual Inversion*—only to be reduced to an uncredited appendix in subsequent editions before finally disappearing from the volume entirely.

52. Richard Burton, "Terminal Essay," in *The Thousand and One Nights*, mimeograph (London, 1901), 3.

53. It may be important to note that Wilde's first literary genre was the fairy tale, which, in his hands, became much like an Oriental parable or a medieval *fabliau* or *nouvel*. That is, Wilde uses the older forms of narrative storytelling in most of these tales rather than a form closer to the modern short story. Quite possibly, Wilde was copying Oriental or Eastern models when doing this.

54. "This so-called 'Sotadic Zone' was named . . . after the Alexandrian poet Sotades (third century BC) whose apparently innocuous verses became obscene if read backward." Rudi C. Bleys, *The Geography of Perversion: Male-to-Male Sexual Behaviour outside the West and the Ethnographic Imagination, 1750–1918* (New York: New York University Press, 1995), 217.

55. Burton, "Terminal Essay," 5.

56. See also the discussion of Burton in Eve Kosofsky Sedgwick, *Between Men: English Literature and Male Homosocial Desire* (New York: Columbia University Press, 1985), 182–83.

57. Burton, "Terminal Essay," 11.

58. Ibid., 12, 17; and in n. 61 (xviii).

59. John Addington Symonds, untitled essay, in *The Sotadic Zone*, by Richard Burton (Boston: Longwood, 1977), 105.

60. Burton, "Terminal Essay," 16.

61. Wilde was at one time a Freemason.

62. Burton, "Terminal Essay," 36.

63. Ibid., 56–57.

64. Ibid., xx n. 67.

65. Symonds, untitled essay, 106.

3. Performing Wilde

1. Quoted in Wayne Koestenbaum, "Wilde's Hard Labor and the Birth of Gay Reading," in *Engendering Men*, ed. Joseph Boone and Michael Cadden (New York: Routledge, 1990), 183.

2. Richard Ellmann, *Oscar Wilde* (New York: Knopf, 1988), 571.

3. See Sedgwick: "So little is this transgressive *practice* [of Bunberrying] seen as tied to the modern homosexual *type*, that Wilde doesn't even confine its attribution to his own gender: the same Gwendolen who's dangerously attracted to effeminate men is also, and apparently *not* as part of the same rhetoric, ascribed an eager anal sexuality that nothing in turn-of-the century (and little enough in contemporary) sexological 'common sense' could have made any space for." "Tales of the Avunculate: Queer Tutelage in *The Importance of Being Earnest*," in *Tendencies* (Durham: Duke University Press, 1993), 68.

4. John Stokes, *In the Nineties* (Chicago: University of Chicago Press, 1989), 137.

5. Oscar Wilde, *The Picture of Dorian Gray*, ed. Peter Ackroyd (New York: Penguin, 1985), 221.

6. Oscar Wilde, "The Ballad of Reading Gaol," in *The Complete Works of Oscar Wilde* (1963; New York: Hamlyn, 1986), 733.

7. Oscar Wilde, "The Harlot's House," in *The Complete Works of Oscar Wilde* (1963; New York: Hamlyn, 1986), 695.

8. Oscar Wilde, "The Critic as Artist," in *The Artist as Critic: Critical Writings of Oscar Wilde*, ed. Richard Ellmann (Chicago: University of Chicago Press, 1969), 361.

9. I am referring again to Sedgwick's "Tales of the Avunculate." See, for example, her claim that in the play "nothing doesn't pay off; almost literally, not a word of the play fails to contribute its full quantum to the clockwork mechanisms of syntactic and semantic parsimony and hyper-salience" (69). Also important here is Sedgwick's discussion of the queer version of "family" created in the play.

10. For more on the construction of bodies in Deleuze's philosophy, see Michael Hardt's discussion of Deleuze and Spinoza in *Gilles Deleuze: An Apprenticeship in Philosophy* (Minneapolis: University of Minnesota Press, 1993), 92.

11. Gilles Deleuze, *Negotiations, 1972–1990*, trans. Martin Joughin (New York: Columbia University Press, 1995), 17.

12. In moving from the imagery of "The Harlot's House" to that of *Earnest*, Wilde's concept of the mechanical body seems to undergo a metamorphosis much like the change in the concept of the body without organs from its first appearance in *Anti-Oedipus* to its later reemergence in *A Thousand Plateaus* (*Mille*

Plateaux). One might argue that the mechanization of the body that we see in *Earnest*—and that seems to have at least one apotheosis in the 1970s clone—is realized most fully in the earlier *Salomé*. Certainly that play, where repetition is central to the use of dialogue, furthers the idea of the mechanical in human form by making dance the central motif (Rhonda K. Garelick, *Rising Star: Dandyism, Gender, and Performance in the Fin de Siècle* [Princeton: Princeton University Press, 1998], 90). The idea that actors might behave like marionettes is probably one that came to Wilde via French theater. Wilde's knowledge of Alfred Jarry's plays is shown in his letters and has been discussed by John Stokes, among others, as an interest that Jarry and Wilde shared (as did Beardsley). John Stokes, *Oscar Wilde: Myths, Miracles, and Imitations* (Cambridge: Cambridge University Press, 1996), 174.

13. Wilde's transvaluing of the mechanical body (the puppet) from something negative in "The Harlot's House" and its other versions to something potentially positive in *Earnest* needs to be seen in light of the idea of the dandy as puppet—an image especially evident in the French literary tradition (Garelick, *Rising Star*, 19).

14. Guy Hocquenghem, *Homosexual Desire*, trans. Daniella Dangoor, with an introduction by Michael Moon (1978; Durham: Duke University Press, 1993), 65.

15. As Hocquenghem notes, "Narcissism is objectless desire, and therefore close to the original libido, and is also this same desire as the absence of a history of the libido. It is the end of the unconsciousness of non-human sex, and the beginning of personalised and imaginary Oedipal sexuality. That is why it stands at the knot of the Oedipalisation of homosexual desire. The body-in-pieces anxiety, the castration anxiety, can obviously only be subsequent to Lacan's 'mirror stage.' To identify oneself, to bind the organs into a single person, means to leave behind the polymorphously perverse or rather to initiate the perversity of the polymorphous. Certainly, the whole person created by the mirror stage comes chronologically second; but actually it comes first, because it is that person who retrospectively gives the first stage its meaning, and all the 'component drives' are then integrated in a bodily unity, according to the principle that the form is pre-existent to the parts. The whole person becomes the absence which is present in the component objects. The search for a counterpart similar to oneself presupposes the existence of the similar and the different" (ibid., 80–81).

16. Ibid., 95.

17. Ibid., 97.

18. Quentin Crisp—perhaps the most famous inheritor of Wilde's type—has been among the many men to play this role.

19. Sedgwick, *Tendencies*, 63.

20. Ibid., 72.

21. Hocquenghem, *Homosexual Desire*, 103.

22. "It has always struck me as curious . . . that when actors rehearse an Oscar Wilde play something happens to them. Usually actors . . . are monsters of egotism. The director's work is initially bent on reforming what the actor perceived as an extension of his or her own personality into something resembling a characterization. But with Wilde it is different. From the start of . . . rehearsals, there was an anxiety about what Wilde would have wanted, how he would have this spoken or that played, as if he were in the back row listening. The sense of his presence in his own plays is overwhelming." Alan Stanford, "Acting Wilde," in *Wilde the Irishman*, ed. Jerusha McCormack (New Haven: Yale University Press, 1998), 156.

23. Lawrence Danson, *Wilde's Intentions: The Artist in His Criticism* (Oxford: Clarendon, 1997), 4.

24. Hocquenghem, *Homosexual Desire*, 114.

25. Sos Eltis, *Revising Wilde: Society and Subversion in the Plays of Oscar Wilde* (Oxford: Clarendon, 1996), 195.

26. Ibid., 197.

27. See Darko Suvin, "The Social Addresses of Victorian Fiction: A Preliminary Enquiry," *Literature and History* 8, no. 1 (1982): 11–40. For more on the fragility of the emerging middle-class identity in Victorian England, see Ed Cohen, *Talk on the Wilde Side: Toward a Genealogy of a Discourse on Male Sexualities* (New York: Routledge, 1993).

28. Laurel Brake's *Subjected Knowledges* contains an important discussion of the changes made by Wilde at *The Woman's World*: gossip is taken seriously; male models are used for women's clothes; a down-market readership is targeted, but higher intelligence is assumed; subjects are expanded to include "masculine" realms; generally, the magazine becomes more progressive while also more savvy economically. See Laurel Brake, *Subjugated Knowledges: Journalism, Gender, and Literature in the Nineteenth Century* (New York: New York University Press, 1994).

29. In fact, a common theme in Wilde's letters from the 1880s until his death in 1900 is his sustained interest in money. Wilde's only living grandchild, Merlin Holland, has updated Rupert Hart-Davis's two collections of Wilde's letters and included many that demonstrate Wilde's networking and money worries—letters that had previously gone unpublished because they were considered repetitive and tedious. I had already noted a number of these on file not only at Texas but at Oxford, Yale, and the British Museum as well and commend Holland for publishing them in full. Wilde's attention to finances runs from the period of his North American tour, when he attempted to get a Catholic publisher in Boston to bring out a U.S. edition of his mother's poems (365), to the end of his life, when he frequently wrote to Frank Harris or his publisher Leonard Smithers requesting five or ten pounds with which to pay his hotel bill. Indeed, his letters end sadly with squabbles and requests for money he felt he was owed. Mixed in with the pleas and threats are letters that also show his attention to the textual editing and design of his final publications, with comments that frequently suggest that he remained well aware of changes in his public persona even after his imprisonment. If anything, Small may underestimate Wilde's constant attention to money. *The Complete Letters of Oscar Wilde*, ed. Merlin Holland and Rupert Hart-Davis (New York: Henry Holt, 2001).

30. In his *Oscar Wilde Revalued*, Small condenses the argument of his article thus: "The 'new' Wilde is occupied less by the brilliant salon life of the 1890s and much more by hard and sometimes rather prosaic work. Wilde becomes the epitome of the new type of professional writer at the turn of the century, concerned with the unglamorous business of self-promotion, negotiating with publishers, cultivating potential reviewers, and constantly polishing his work. Moreover his interests are now seen to be much more wide-ranging than those associated with the literary and art worlds of the time. The 'new' Wilde is preoccupied with issues such as authority, gender, identity, and prison reform; he is seen as thoroughly and seriously engaged with some of the most contentious intellectual issues of his day." *Oscar Wilde Revalued: An Essay on New Methods and Methods of Research* (Greensboro: ELT, 1993), 31.

31. Cf. Cohen: "Even as one of the first and, indeed, most successful nineteenth-century men to self-consciously market himself as cultural icon, without the trials Wilde would never have achieved (in the days before *People* magazine) the ubiquitous coverage that derived from his 'downfall'" (*Talk on the Wilde Side*, 101).

32. Stokes credits Wilde with joining "the Paterian emphasis on 'being' [with] Baudelaire's idea of the Dandy to supply a definition of the artist." John Stokes, *Oscar Wilde* (Burnt Mill, Harlow, Essex: Longman, 1978), 19. For Wilde, in other words, being became the ultimate aim of art; hence autobiography—or personality—was the final goal of any artist. Style was not separate from the artist; rather, style was personality—and vice versa.

33. Wilde's own comments about the importance of the concept of type and personality are illuminating here. He talks about the idea of a type in relation to personality and autobiography in "The English Renaissance of Art," "Pen, Pencil, and Poison," "The Portrait of Mr. W. H.," "The Decay of Lying," and "The Critic as Artist." See, for example, the following from "Pen, Pencil, and Poison": "He also saw that it was quite easy by continued reiteration to make the public interested in his own personality, and in his purely journalistic arti-cles this extraordinary young man tells the world what he had for dinner, where he gets his clothes, what wines he likes, and in what state of health he is, just as if he were writing weekly notes for some popular newspaper of our own time. This being the least valuable side of his work, is the one that has had the most obvious influence. A publicist, nowadays, is a man who bores the community with the details of the illegalities of his private life." Oscar Wilde, "Pen, Pencil, and Poison," in *The Artist as Critic: Critical Writings of Oscar Wilde*, ed. Richard Ellmann (Chicago: University of Chicago Press, 1969), 332.

34. Arthur Conan Doyle, "A Golden Evening," in *Oscar Wilde: Interviews and Recollections*, ed. E. H. Mikhail, vol. 1 (New York: Barnes and Noble, 1979), 161.

35. Adolphe Retté, "Salomé," in *Oscar Wilde: Interviews and Recollections*, ed. E. H. Mikhail, vol. 1 (New York: Barnes and Noble, 1979), 190.

36. A. J. A. Symons, "The Diner-Out," in *Oscar Wilde: Interviews and Recollec-tions*, ed. E. H. Mikhail, vol. 1 (New York: Barnes and Noble, 1979), 175.

37. William Butler Yeats, *The Autobiography of William Butler Yeats* (New York: Collier, 1965), 90.

38. Richard Le Gallienne, "Oscar Wilde as a Symbolic Figure," in *Oscar Wilde: Interviews and Recollections*, ed. E. H. Mikhail, vol. 2 (New York: Barnes and Noble, 1979), 397. Cf. Miller: "By the time of his imprisonment, Wilde had come to look upon his own life as a form of artistic expression, as if he were for-ever a figure upon a public stage." Robert Keith Miller, *Oscar Wilde* (New York: Frederick Ungar, 1982), 122.

39. Cf. Small in *Revalued*: "In the case of Wilde, the notion of the 'sage' has now given way to that of the prototypical media 'personality' created by, and for, an emerging consumerist culture" (151).

40. Henri de Régnier, "Oscar Wilde," in *Oscar Wilde: Interviews and Recollections*, ed. E. H. Mikhail, vol. 2 (New York: Barnes and Noble, 1979), 464.

41. Laurence Housman, *Echo de Paris* (New York: D. Appleton, 1924).

42. Compare the description Winwar gives of Wilde in exile and note how he is both a character in a play and the author of it twenty years after Housman was writing: "There was nothing that Wilde, talking, could not accomplish. The beautiful prose poems, each word of which fit into the pattern of language like a well-cut jewel, still marked him the meticulous artist. The plays which he could not get himself to write enacted themselves before his listeners, scene following scene, as Wilde took now one part, now the other, his face and voice changing in masterly mimicry in the scintillating dialogue he had not the will power to set down. Stories of Christ, imagined events that the Gospels might well have recorded, sounded above the clatter of the *garçons* busy with their trays and glasses." Frances Winwar, *Oscar Wilde and the Yellow Nineties* (Garden City, N.Y.: Blue Ribbon Books, 1940), 355.

43. Instances of Wilde's reemergence throughout the twentieth century as a fictional or semifictional character are too numerous to list. Some examples include Godfrey W. Mathews, *The Madonna of Montmartre: A Story Oscar Wilde Never Told* ("Printed for Private Circulation," Liverpool: E. A. Bryant, 1930); and John Furnell, *The Stringed Lute: An Evocation in Dialogue of Oscar Wilde*, (London: Rider, 1955).

44. Avrom Fleishman, *Figures of Autobiography: The Language of Self-Writing in Victorian and Modern England* (Berkeley: University of California Press, 1983), 286.

45. Ibid., 292.

46. Michael Anton Budd notes that Sarony photographed not only Wilde but also the muscled Eugen Sandow, who was also "engaged in the same commercial activity of selling a photographically manufactured self. But Wilde's body was hidden beneath clothes and Sandow's was undressed for all to see. In further comparing the two, however, a reversal takes place in which the nearly nude Sandow stands as the more opaque figure while the pallid and lank young Wilde fully dressed and in lace cuffs appears as the more transparent." Michael Anton

Budd, *The Sculpture Machine: Physical Culture and Body Politics in the Age of Empire* (New York: New York University Press, 1997), 73.

47. Jane M. Gaines, *Contested Culture: The Image, the Voice, and the Law* (Chapel Hill: University of North Carolina Press, 1991), 81.

48. In two separate letters of 1898 to Smithers and to George Ives, Wilde writes that a new advertisement for *The Ballad of Reading Gaol* that proclaims "3,000 copies sold in three weeks" makes him "feel like Lipton's tea!" Wilde seems to enjoy here the process of imagining himself as a popular commodity. In the earlier letter, Wilde also mentions "Pears' soap, and other more useful things." Oscar Wilde, "To Leonard Smithers," March 20, 1898, in Holland and Hart-Davis, *Complete Letters*, 1043; Oscar Wilde, "To George Ives," March 21, 1898, ibid., 1044.

49. Gaines, *Contested Culture*, 73.

50. "Especially popular in the 1860s and 70s, the carte-de-visite was eventually phased out by magazine reproduction and cameras for individual use (which eliminated the necessity for studio photography). The vast majority (close to 90%) of cartes-de-visite were portraits, and the mass market for these photographs, which people collected and made into albums, was dominated by celebrities, especially from the theater. So profitable were the sales of cartes-de-visite that one of the most successful photographers, Napoleon Sarony, who was noted for his ability to create dramatic portraits of actors and actresses, began to pay celebrities to pose for him. Sarah Bernhardt, for example, was paid $1,500 to pose for a photograph. Eager to capitalize on this form of publicity, when Oscar Wilde toured the U.S. in 1882, he posed for free." Ann Cvetkovich, "Histories of Mass Culture: From Literary to Visual Culture," *Victorian Literature and Culture* 27, no. 2 (1999): 497.

51. Gaines, *Contested Culture*, 59.

52. Reva Wolf notes that in the 1960s, Warhol created double portraits that were similar to carte-de-visite photographs made in the 1860s by actress Adah Isaacs Menken in which she "posed with famous men . . . in ways that elicited public gossip about what precisely her relationship with each of the two men was." Warhol's double portraits created similar "social discourse." Reva Wolf, *Andy Warhol, Poetry, and Gossip in the 1960s* (Chicago: University of Chicago Press, 1997), 28.

53. "Clearly the mass reproduction of the photograph that enabled the

carte-de-visite also enabled a particular form of fan culture—the collection of images of the celebrity, whose public status was significantly visual. Charting the shift from the carte-de-visite, an individually sold image, to magazines, which were a possible source for scrapbooks and cut-out pin-ups, produces a material history that has the potential to answer larger questions about the intersections of consumerism and sexual identities and the politics of visibility" (Cvetkovich, "Histories of Mass Culture," 497).

4. Talking as Performance

1. Oscar Wilde, "The Soul of Man under Socialism," in *The Artist as Critic: Critical Writings of Oscar Wilde*, ed. Richard Ellmann (Chicago: University of Chicago Press, 1969), 276.

2. Compare the following from Briggs: "The year 1896, when Lord Northcliffe founded the *Daily Mail*, was also the year when Oscar Wilde started his prison sentence, a critical date in the story of the late-Victorian revolt. In the same year young Marconi arrived in London to sell his wireless inventions to the Post Office and the first cinema show was presented in the West End, a critical date in modern social and cultural history." Asa Briggs, *Victorian Cities* (London: Odhams Books, 1963), 368.

3. Truman Capote, *The Dogs Bark: Public People and Private Places* (New York: New American Library, 1973), xi.

4. Ibid., xii.

5. Wilde's delight in gossip was perhaps complicated by his relationship to journalism, though he drew on both for his problem plays. From *Lady Windermere* through *Earnest*, Wilde assumed that his audience would be able to pick up the allusions not only to current events and issues but also to gossip and rumors. Showing his indebtedness to Zola and Ibsen, Wilde practiced his own version of what would later—in the hands of someone like Tom Wolfe—be called a "New Journalism." Wilde's mixing of genres and styles—his application of fictional or dramatic techniques to material that was popular or even subversive—was prescient precisely because it foretold two different developments: the further collapse of genres after World War II, when novels could become nonfiction and journalistic articles could be labeled artistic, and the centrality of queer forms of knowing to the literary experimentation of the twentieth century.

6. Canadian writer Timothy Findley explores this milieu in his novel *The Wars* (1978). Sharing much with Capote's unfinished novel, Findley's masterpiece follows a young Canadian soldier through World War I as he begins to explore his sexuality. The novel is filled with references to Wilde's first male lover and his executor, Robbie Ross, as well as to Sassoon and Owens—both of whom seem to be referenced as the model for the novel's young protagonist.

7. Lawrence Grobel, *Conversations with Capote* (New York: New American Library, 1985), 146.

8. The theme of Capote's masked ball was the Arabian Nights. Gerald Clarke, *Capote: A Biography* (New York: Simon, 1988), 510.

9. Ibid., 315.

10. See Mailer's *Of a Small and Modest Malignancy, Wicked and Bristling with Dots* (Northridge: Lord John, 1980).

11. Compare Capote's comments to Steinem in response to a question about whether there is "something to be learned from them [Beautiful People]": "The freedom to pursue an esthetic quality in life is an extra dimension. . . . Why not create a whole esthetic ambience? Be your own living work of art?" Gloria Steinem, "'Go Right Ahead and Ask Me Anything' (And She Did): An Interview with Truman Capote," in *Truman Capote: Conversations*, ed. M. Thomas Inge (Jackson: University Press of Mississippi, 1987), 90.

12. Truman Capote, *Music for Chameleons* (New York: Random, 1980), xviii.

13. Ibid.

14. Ibid.

15. Ibid., 196.

16. Capote, *The Dogs Bark*, xiv.

17. Capote, *Music for Chameleons*, 261.

18. Compare the following from Ryals's biography of Browning: "Browning was born, but 'Browning' was scripted over a period of many years. Relying chiefly on his own theatrical metaphors, I portray the poet as he depicted himself: as both the presenter and the presented. I assume that each of his works is what he himself called it—a performance—and that he produced and enacted it as part of a (biographical) script that was subject to constant modification." Clyde de L. Ryals, *The Life of Robert Browning: A Critical Biography* (Cambridge: Blackwell, 1993), ix.

19. Capote's collection is termed "postmodern" by Jack Hicks, who claims

that Capote wanted to disrupt the smooth realist surface of *In Cold Blood* by "a variety of postmodern traits," which include "Capote's pastiche of diary extracts and dramatic scaffoldings, and an insistent, interrupting parenthetical style. Such devices jar the plates of social realism, bare the artifice of the narrative scope, insist on the textuality and intertextuality of setting, character, and plot." Jack Hicks, "'Fire, Fire, Fire Flowing like a River, River, River': History and Postmodernism in Truman Capote's *Handcarved Coffins*," in *The Critical Response to Truman Capote*, ed. Joseph J. Waldmeir and John C. Waldmeir (Westport, Conn.: Greenwood, 1999), 171. That Capote would not attempt the successful technique of *In Cold Blood* should not come as a surprise from a writer who was often considered to have mastered the formal techniques of various genres before *In Cold Blood*. More likely, perhaps, is the idea that Capote had finally bested himself in, as he claimed, inventing a genre—the "nonfiction novel"—and now attempting to do that again, but with limited success.

20. Fouts's amazing beauty never waned before he died of a heart attack at the age of thirty-five. Clarke claims that "Oscar Wilde had written his biography before Denny was born: Denny was Dorian Gray" (173).

21. Jones describes the Vicomtesse Marie Laure de Noailles as an "esteemed poet, a *saloniste* who presided over a drawing room where the ectoplasmic presences of Proust and Reynaldo Hahn were at any moment expected to materialize," and as having a "middle-parted coiffure that eerily duplicated Lautrec's portrait of Oscar Wilde" (37).

22. Capote was later to dedicate *Music for Chameleons* to Williams, who was less than gracious in acknowledging it.

23. Capote says of *Answered Prayers*, "I don't consider my book gossip at all. But then, all conversation is gossip. Every novel that you've ever read is nothing but gossip, but it depends on what level of artistry it's done on." Truman Capote, interview, *Scavullo on Men*, by Francesco Scavullo and Bob Colacello (New York: Random, 1977), 56.

24. Truman Capote, *Answered Prayers: The Unfinished Novel* (New York: New American Library, 1987), 48.

25. Ibid.

26. Ibid., 34.

27. Ibid., 33.

28. Ibid., 34.

29. As Capote notes at the time of the *Esquire* serialization, "I've been very interested in almost all of the writers who have been writing about my book. They have read the chapters published . . . and they really are very excited about it—because it *is* completely different. And that's one of the things that really excites them, that I have the actual nerve to do this, aside from the technical skill and ability—it's a kind of moral breakthrough" (Capote interview, *Scavullo on Men*, 56).

30. Thanks to John Evelev for this insight and his help in thinking through *Answered Prayers*. Some of the thoughts here are surely his, too.

31. James A. Michener, foreword to *Conversations with Capote*, by Lawrence Grobel (New York: New American Library, 1985), 2.

32. Michener later says, "Byron was a Truman Capote of his day" (9).

33. James A. Michener, "Playboy Interview," *Playboy*, September 1981, 90.

34. Grobel, *Conversations with Capote*, 91.

35. Ibid., 92.

36. John Knowles, "Musings on a Chameleon," *Esquire*, April 1988, 182.

37. Dir. Robert Moore.

38. See Capote's comments on the film in his interview in *Scavullo on Men*, 57, which were typical of the comments he made about the experience of making the film.

39. For Capote, see the murder mystery *Dear Mr. Capote* and the one-man show *Tru*; for Wilde, one could take the recent example of Eagleton's play *Saint Oscar*.

40. Andy Warhol, "Sunday with Mister C.: An Audiodocumentary by Andy Warhol Starring Truman Capote," in *Truman Capote: Conversations*, ed. M. Thomas Inge (Jackson: University Press of Mississippi, 1987), 266.

41. Andy Warhol and Pat Hackett, *Popism: The Warhol Sixties* (New York: Harcourt Brace Jovanovitch, 1980), 193; Capote added the following details to the events in one of his conversations with Grobel: "When he was a child, Andy Warhol had this obsession about me and used to write me from Pittsburgh, when he was a high-school student. When he came to New York, he used to stand outside my house, just stand out there all day waiting for me to come out. He wanted to become a friend of mine, wanted to speak to me, to talk to me. He nearly drove me crazy" (187).

42. See Warhol and Hackett, *Popism*, 60–63.

43. According to Reva Wolf, while Warhol was a fan of O'Hara's poetry, O'Hara was critical of Warhol's version of pop art (18).

44. See Bob Colacello, *Holy Terror: Andy Warhol Close Up* (New York: Harper, 1990), 398–406.

45. Cf. Richard Dyer: "Oscar Wilde had been there already. In the preface to *The Picture of Dorian Gray* he wrote of the great virtue of being 'as artificial as possible.' He too was coming at the end of a movement that had concealed its perverse well-springs in a display of splurging emotional authenticity. Not only does Warhol recapitulate the history of Hollywood, the underground recapitulates the history of romanticism and decadence, as well as that history, which echoes it, of modernism and postmodernism." Richard Dyer, *Now You See It: Studies on Lesbian and Gay Film* (New York: Routledge, 1990), 154. Warhol's films would eventually adopt more 'sophisticated' cinematic techniques such as the pan and zoom, but only under the influence of Paul Morrissey.

46. Warhol, "Sunday with Mister C.," 291.

47. Warhol attributes this epigram to Franco Rossellini.

48. Andy Warhol, *The Philosophy of Andy Warhol: (From A to B and Back Again)* (New York: Harcourt Brace Jovanovitch, 1975), 53.

49. *Superstar: The Life and Times of Andy Warhol*, dir. Chuck Workman, 1991.

50. Andrew Ross, *No Respect: Intellectuals and Popular Culture* (New York: Routledge, 1989), 170.

51. Frith and Howard Horne observe that "one strand of Warhol's argument was that 'real' art's claim to be somehow non-commercial, to be based on aesthetic principles that transcend the market place, is bunkum—and part of Warhol's 'radical' effect was simply to draw attention to the high art market. . . . 'Real' art is defined simply by the taste (and wealth) of the ruling class of the period. This implies not only that commercial art is just as good as 'real' art—its value simply being defined by other social groups, other patterns of expenditure but, also, that in democratic terms it is better, representing popular rather than elite taste." Simon Frith and Howard Horne, *Art into Pop* (New York: Methuen, 1987), 109. Ross argues more harshly that after his shooting, "Warhol moved . . . from . . . hustlers, junkies, drag queens—to the world of Andy Warhol Enterprises. . . . In this latter phase, he played at being a hired flunky in the same way as he had earlier played at being a tastemaker for the East Coast trash aesthetic. His diabolical reputation, in the media, for making money out

of everything he did, no matter what role he was playing, was the punishment for the way in which he called attention to the contradictory logic of publicity culture, provoking not only the envious magnates of the mass media, but also the anti-commercial conscience of the counterculture. But whether or not Warhol acted out his role in order to expose the process of exploitation, was finally irrelevant. He was no more an opponent of the process than he was a traditional legitimist for the power and prestige of the glitterati. The point was always to ask: What's art got to do with it?" (169).

52. Capote's last great anecdote that he often retold was about a moment of wit that came upon him while dining in a crowded restaurant in Key West, Florida, with Tennessee Williams. As the story goes, Capote was approached by a woman who asked that he autograph one of her breasts. Capote was happy to oblige. A few minutes later, the woman's husband came up to the two writers, took out his penis, and exclaimed, "While you're at it, why don't you sign this!" Capote retorted, "Well, maybe I can initial it." Variations of this story appeared on television, in published interviews, and finally in Capote's last piece of journalism, "Remembering Tennessee." In some versions of the story, Capote autographs the woman's stomach rather than her breast, and in one, Capote's lover of the time, Jack O'Shea, is the one with the clever retort. In any case, Capote inserts the story into various contexts—for several years—before he uses it as the comic relief in his obituary for Williams.

53. While Warhol's own *Torso* and *Piss* series (1977) allude to the homoerotic themes of his own prepop periods, they may be an allusion to a younger generation of gay painters like Hockney, as well.

54. E.g., *David Hockney by David Hockney*, ed. Nikos Stangos (New York: Harry N. Abrams, 1976).

55. Jack Babuscio, "Camp and the Gay Sensibility," in *Camp Grounds: Style and Homosexuality*, ed. David Bergman (Amherst: University of Massachusetts Press, 1993), 43.

5. Phenomenology of Performance

1. Allan Kaprow, "Notes on the Creation of a Total Art," in *Essays on the Blurring of Art and Life* (Berkeley: University of California Press, 1993), 61–62.

2. "Put together out of taped conversations between Andy and Brigid Polk by Anthony Ingrassia of the Theater of the Ridiculous, *Pork* centered on the

curious character of one 'B. Marlowe' (Andy) as he taped the scatological comments and snapped the obscene poses of 'Amanda Pork' (Brigid), 'Vulva' (Viva, played by a transvestite), and the 'Pepsodent Twins,' two nude boys with pastel-powdered genitals (based on Jay and Jed Johnson)." Victor Bockris, *The Life and Death of Andy Warhol* (New York: Bantam, 1989), 263.

3. Brian Eno, who was originally a member of Brian Ferry's Roxy Music, was one, and Pete Townshend was another. John Lennon, a frustrated artist, did not complete art school but shared the same desire to work in multiple media. Bowie was himself a part of the ill-fated Beckenham Arts Lab, though even an arts lab was too close to a go-as-you-will hippie concept for Bowie.

4. The question of Bowie's appeal within and across lines of class and gender is a complex one. Bowie's attraction is surely available for people who are not middle-class, as Bowie's influence on punk aesthetics was formative, and punk's power base was not middle-class. Some would claim, however, that at least in Britain, Bowie's widespread appeal would never have been possible without the dawning television culture, which was at that time decidedly middle-class. Certainly Bowie's own aesthetic appeal, like Warhol's, had much to do with consumption. Yet I am not ready to dismiss his possible importance to the working class even if Bowie's own desire to break free from suburbia fueled much of his early music. As for gender, a pre-1980s feminist take on Bowie might argue that the androgyny that he displayed in his earlier personae was simply not available to his young female fans. And yet, as I hope to go on to show, I am not sure that androgyny in the sense of cross-dressing is really what was at work in Bowie. Instead, one should note that Bowie fans have often been girls—even if it was originally the male fans' gender-bending looks that caught the media's eye. The whole question of race, which is anything but a footnote here, is a topic that has been dealt with less often, though one that is ripe for research. Just to name the most obvious starting points: Bowie's "Fame" was not only influential in black disco circles but provided him with the honor of being the first white singer to perform on *Soul Train*; the connection between techno music and African sounds was one that Bowie helped to foster with his Berlin trilogy of albums; Bowie's long association with African American musicians, such as rhythm guitarist Carlos Alomar, and producers, such as Nile Rodgers, shows up in the frequency with which one can hear the influence of rhythm and blues in his work since the mid-1970s.

5. Elizabeth Pincus, "Bowie 2000," *Out*, October 1995, 130.

6. Not to mention groups whose members are either definitely out—Pansy Division—or who play with sexual ambiguity such as Blur.

7. Apparently Kemp tried to stage a production of Genet's *The Maids*, but it was closed down. He did go on in the seventies to perform his own version of *Salomé* and to create *Flowers . . . A Pantomime for Jean Genet*.

8. Derek Jarman, foreword to *Lindsay Kemp and Company* (London: GMP, 1987), 6.

9. Ibid.

10. See David A. Keeps, "I'm David Bowie and You're Not," *Details* (Winter 1995): 173: "My choices are made from the shirt that I wear—which will describe something about my fantasy of how my day will be—to the chair I sit in. *(points to a hideous pink club chair)* I would not pick that chair today. Why not? Because I don't have an empathy with what it represents. I will choose a chair that maybe has a kind of Bauhaus feel because I feel today that represents my very focused and clear perspective. I create my culture daily, we all do. That's part of the excitement of being alive." Bowie's somewhat pedagogical declamation here points to a new wave of somewhat-intellectual pop cult studs practiced by the performers themselves: Eno is now a professor in England; David Duchovny, star of television's *The X-Files*, is ABD in English from Yale; Bowie quotes Camille Paglia in another essay.

11. Dir. Malcolm J. Thompson, 1969.

12. In some ways Bowie's most famous alter ego, Iggy Pop, has been one of his more elaborate masks. The raw-edged, protopunk musician from Detroit is the antithesis of the suave Londoner. Yet the two have collaborated on writing songs for each other's albums—*The Idiot* (1977), *Lust for Life* (1977), *Let's Dance*, and *Tonight* (1984)—and Bowie has produced Pop's albums in the seventies and in the eighties. Indeed, during the 1980s, when Bowie's own artistic successes were few, his collaborative work on Pop's *Blah Blah Blah* (1986) represented some of his best work in the decade.

13. John Rechy, *City of Night* (New York: Grove, 1963). Rechy's novel might serve as a source for some of the atmosphere that Bowie uses in *Aladdin Sane*. The subtitle to the title track, "(1913–1938–197?)," suggests periods of decadence between the wars in Europe. Mike Garson's piano work, which dominates the album, is a haunted player piano whose sound suggests a nostalgia for a

former age not dominated by war or strife. The futuristic setting of the album, therefore, is offset by the album's evocation of the 1920s—not unlike Lou Reed's *Berlin*. Rechy's novel, which evokes similar textures, but of the underground gay world of the United States, may be the bridge that linked twenties Berlin and contemporary America in Bowie's mind. His most sustained discourse on "decadence," *Aladdin Sane*'s landscapes can be seen reflected in Rechy's prose: "Later I would think of America as one vast City of Night stretching gaudily from Times Square to Hollywood Boulevard—jukebox-winking, rock-n-roll moaning: America at night fusing its darkcities into the unmistakable shape of loneliness" (11). Even as late as the lyrics to *Low*, Bowie may still have Rechy in mind. Compare Rechy's "But in the Southwest, the sky was millions and millions of miles deep of blue—clear, magic, electric blue" (12) to Bowie's reference to "electric blue" in the lyrics to "Sound and Vision." Likewise, Rechy creates his own references to Dorian Gray, a favorite trope of Bowie's and of gay writers in the twentieth century: "From my father's inexplicable hatred of me and my mother's blind carnivorous love, I fled to the Mirror. I would stand before it, thinking: I have only Me! . . . I became obsessed with age. At 17, I dreaded growing old. Old age is something that must never happen to me. The image of myself in the mirror must never fade into someone I cant look at" (21).

14. In a recent interview, Bowie says, "I was very aware of the idea of androgyny or an unknown gender being attached to most priesthoods in the East." Ingrid Sischy, "David Bowie," *Interview*, September 1995, 157.

15. For Wilde's own take on costuming and clothes, see "The Truth of Masks," where his claims for the importance of costuming are made by his attempting to prove that Shakespeare understood it and took it very seriously: "until an actor is at home in his dress, he is not at home in his part." See Oscar Wilde, "The Truth of Masks," in *The Artist as Critic: Critical Writings of Oscar Wilde*, ed. Richard Ellmann (Chicago: University of Chicago Press, 1969), 431.

16. However, as Bowie was to go on to show, his costumes—which he usually wore offstage as well as on—did continue to reflect the silhouette and shape, if not always the decoration and materials, that would usually belong to women's clothing rather than to men's. As the Thin White Duke in the mid-seventies, he dressed in black vests and pants mainly borrowed from Dietrich, who was herself borrowing from her role in *The Blue Angel* (1930). Likewise, at least until the end of the seventies, Bowie's concert costumes either took directly from gay styles—his sailor's outfit for his 1978 "Heroes" World Tour, for instance—or

continued to emphasize not only an obviously made-up face but also pants and shirts whose lines were cut more like women's clothes of the 1930s than the costumes that he would wear in the next two decades that referenced traditional masculine styles.

17. John Gill, "Dire Straights: Ziggy, Iggy, Marc, Lou," in *Queer Noises: Male and Female Homosexuality in Twentieth-Century Music* (Minneapolis: University of Minnesota Press, 1995), 110.

18. Ibid.

19. Jarman, foreword, 5.

20. Theodore Gracyk, *Rhythm and Noise: An Aesthetics of Rock* (Durham: Duke University Press, 1996), 53.

21. Ibid., 81.

22. Simon Frith, *Performing Rites: On the Value of Popular Music* (Cambridge: Harvard University Press, 1996), 204.

23. Ibid., 205.

24. Jane M. Gaines, *Contested Culture: The Image, the Voice, and the Law* (Chapel Hill: University of North Carolina Press, 1991), 116.

25. Susan McClary, *Feminine Endings: Music, Gender, Sexuality* (Minneapolis: University of Minnesota Press, 1991).

26. Roland Barthes, "The Grain of the Voice," in *Image/Music/Text*, trans. Stephen Heath (New York: Hill and Wang, 1977), 181.

27. Paul E. Willis, *Common Culture: Symbolic Work at Play in the Everyday Cultures of the Young* (Boulder: Westview, 1990), 64.

28. Elizabeth Thomson and David Gutman, introduction to *The Bowie Companion*, ed. Elizabeth Thomson and David Gutman (London: Macmillan, 1993), xxx.

29. Ian Penman, "The Shattered Glass: Notes on Bryan Ferry," in *Zoot Suits and Second-Hand Dresses*, ed. Angel McRobie (Winchester, Mass.: Unwin Hyman, 1988), 111.

30. Likewise, the members of Bowie's band were dressed in various versions of "Oriental" regalia: a fez here, a dashiki there. In the film, this flirtation with the Orient is made ironic, but in a different way.

31. It should be noted that much of Bowie's ability to turn in a performance here that is not only top-notch but also remarkably unusual may not have been possible were it not for the discipline—and perhaps confidence—that he achieved in his portrayal of the deformed John Merrick in Bernard Pomerance's *The*

Elephant Man. Bowie took over the role for the 1980–1981 run on Broadway and won rave critical reviews for his ability to suggest Merrick's physical condition through his voice and gestures. Dressed in a simple white cloth with a walking stick as his only prop, Bowie appeared without the elaborate makeup that John Hurt would wear for David Lynch's film version.

32. John Mowitt, "Performance Theory as the Work of Laurie Anderson," *Discourse: Theoretical Studies in Media and Culture* 12, no. 2 (Spring–Summer 1990): 54.

33. For more on the breakdown of the differences between writing and other forms of expression, see Mowitt's *Text: The Genealogy of an Antidisciplinary Object* (Durham: Duke University Press, 1992).

34. Joe Gore, "David Bowie and Reeves Gabrels," *Guitar Player* 31, no. 6 (June 1997): 55.

35. Including some of the members of *Pork*, such as Wayne (now Jayne) County and Leee Black Childers.

36. Although Bowie experimented with cabaret elements in his music in an attempt to create atmospheric textures that suggested not only decadence but also vaudeville scenes and dramatics, the only two songs in his entire output that definitely address gay men as characters are "Queen Bitch" from *Hunky Dory* (1972) and "John, I'm Only Dancing," which was written with the songs for that album. The former has been described as being "about the singer's boyfriend being seduced by another queen." Michael Watts, "Oh You Pretty Things," in *The Bowie Companion*, ed. Elizabeth Thomson and David Gutman (London: Macmillan, 1993), 48. The title is a parody of the Velvet Underground, then disbanded, whose tradition was being carried on not only by Bowie but also by Reed, whose own album about decadence, *Berlin*, referenced Isherwood in an attempt to create an opera about transvestite culture. Reed's "Walk on the Wild Side," from the Bowie-produced *Transformer* (1972), is a description of Warhol's retinue of "stars," such as the ravishingly beautiful preoperative transsexual Candy Darling. Bowie's ode to Reed, therefore, was also a reference to the homosexual underground over which Warhol held sway.

37. See especially Simon Frith's "Only Dancing," *Mother Jones* 8, no. 7 (August 1983): 16–22.

38. Andrew Goodwin, *Dancing in the Distraction Factory: Music Television and Popular Culture* (Minneapolis: University of Minnesota Press, 1992), 109.

39. Michael Jarrett, "Concerning the Progress of Rock and Roll," *South Atlantic Quarterly: Rock and Roll Culture*, ed. Anthony DeCurtis 90, no. 4 (Fall 1991): 814.

40. Bowie is one of the first two pop musicians (Prince is the other) to create an interactive CD for his fans.

41. E.g., Josef Woodard, "Getting Low," *Musician*, June 1993, 40–49.

42. Bowie's concept cannot help but reference the interest Wilde had in the fusing of art with crime in "The Portrait of Mr. W. H."

43. "As we get toward the end of the millennium, there's intense interest in the body itself, and Brian [Eno] and I are sort of talking it through and trying to relate to its pagan origins, where the body comes into play in ritualization. Art is definitely going through a 'blood' period at the moment." Tom Lanham, "David Bowie," *CD Review*, October 1995, 32.

44. For more on Athey's work, see John Edward McGrath's "Trusting in Rubber: Performing Boundaries during the AIDS Epidemic." *TDR* 39, no. 2 (Summer 1995): 18–21. McGrath's discussion of Jeff Weiss and Athey's performances point to Weiss's use of "a serial killer" to narrativize AIDS, while Athey "dresses in rubber and leather, wraps himself and others in plastic, whips and is whipped in quasi-religious rituals, and in the final scenes of the work . . . like Christ and then like St. Sebastian his body is pierced onstage in front of you." Indeed, he is pierced with hypodermic needles, which is what the art-criminal uses on the victim in Bowie's album. With lyrics such as "there was nothing between us but your clothes" and "we prick you," Bowie's possible references to AIDS may be an attempt to address Athey's performances. Athey has been known to accompany his performances with techno music. Likewise, Chris Burden has worked with Laurie Anderson. The connection that Bowie might have to this subgenre of performance or conceptual art is perhaps not as strange as it might seem.

45. For all his careful attempts to trace his influences in the world of high art, Bowie's largest indebtedness seems to me to be to the late German conceptual artist Joseph Beuys.

46. Bowie is currently art critic for *Modern Painters* magazine. In an interview with British artist Damien Hirst, Bowie discuss "body-part art" and the relationship between murder and art. David Bowie, "(S)now: David Bowie Interviews Damien Hirst," *Modern Painters* 9 (Summer 1996): 36.

47. There is one direct reference to Bowie's album *Diamond Dogs* in the lyric

"bullet-proof mask." This is sung by the title character on that album and perhaps shows that in writing *Outside*, Bowie was thinking of this album especially. Whereas that album was a staging of Orwell's *1984* as a rock opera/ performance piece, Bowie has here written his own script.

48. Bowie claims that the idea for the album came at least in part from an experiment at the "Guggin mental hospital just outside of Vienna," where mental patients have been allowed to paint. "Some of them don't even do it [painting] as an expression of themselves; they do it because their work *is* them" (Sischy, "David Bowie," 142).

49. Beginning at least with the Beatles' *Sgt. Pepper's*, the concept album was an attempt to blend together various forms of art to move beyond a collection of singles and B-sides. The concept album as a form or musical genre was already an operatic one composed of layers of musical textures, multiple characters or voices, and complex feelings woven together to create an illusion of "depth."

50. Like Kubrick, Bowie seems to be asking his fans to imagine a future that looks back on the present—rather than a present that looks toward (or for) a future.

51. Bowie's vocal performance in *Baal* from 1981 is the most obvious forerunner to much of the singing here.

52. In an online discussion of the album before it was finished, Bowie actually describes it as a CD-ROM project with Eno, even though he also discusses having already recorded "tons of tracks" with Eno, Garson, and others. "Bowie On Line!" ed. Renae Carol Dutkowski, transmitted July 1, 1994, at 05:42:05 EDT. As a concept, the album would perhaps exist best as a Web site or some type of CD-ROM creation, both of which would allow for the merging of the audio, visual, and textual. To some extent this experimentation exists in the David Bowie home page on the Internet (http://www.davidbowie.com), where Bowie elaborates on the album's production history and on its concept, including descriptions of the album's plot and characters: "Ramona A. Stone, a survivor of the seventies, is a second suspect. Her bizarre history of activities equals her sartorial self. A one-time high-priestess of a Berlin-based suicide cult, then proprietress of a body-parts jewelry store in London, the nineties find her underground in Oxford Town, surrounded by her sycophantic coteries of miscreants and acolytes."

53. For example: "Brian [Eno] borrows from pop culture and elevates up—I take from high art and demean it down." Mark Rowland, "The Outside Story," *Musician* 204 (November 1995): 32.

54. In a recent interview, Eno and Bowie talk about pop culture's own self-reference and a generational shift in how culture is assimilated, how "depth" has given way to "surface," and how the hierarchies of low and high have been broken. See Josef Woodard, "Getting Low," *Musician*, June 1993, 40–49.

55. Nick James, "American Voyeur," *Sight and Sound* 8, no. 9 (September 1998): 8.

56. Joel H. Kaplan and Sheila Stowell, *Theatre and Fashion: Oscar Wilde to the Suffragettes* (Cambridge: Cambridge University Press, 1994), 44.

57. Ibid., 218.

Coda

1. Bowie's first manager, Pitt collected first editions of Wilde and Rupert Croft-Cook. An early influence on Bowie parallel to Kemp, *The Ballad of Reading Gaol* was Pitt's favorite work, as he "saw Wilde's bitter epic poem, spelling out the dire consequences of being imprisoned for homosexual behaviour, as a story with powerful modern parallels. Pitt had strong sympathy for the plight of homosexual men in post-war Britain, still stigmatised for their sexual preferences, and still liable, even at the beginning of 1967, to legal penalties for indulging in them." Peter Gillman, *Alias David Bowie: A Biography* (New York: H. Holt, 1986), 131.

2. Frith argues in an essay from 1985 that "pop effects are usually explained in terms of identity—the key words in most pop songs are 'I' and 'You,' and in 'Rock and Sexuality' we suggested that, for the most part, boys identify with the performing 'I,' girls with the addressed 'you.' But once we start looking at pop genres in detail, the play of identity and address becomes rather more complicated. Whether in the teenybop education of desire . . . the Springsteenian community or torch-singing, the best records (the ones that give most pleasure) are the ones that allow an ambiguity of response, letting us be both subject and object of the singers' needs." Simon Frith, *Music for Pleasure: Essays in the Sociology of Pop* (New York: Routledge, 1988), 167.

3. Much thanks to Neil Tennant of the Pet Shop Boys for providing me with his interpretation of the sexual politics of the three songs that I discuss here. My views are certainly my own. Neil Tennant, letter to the author, October 21, 2002. Reviews and articles on the work by the Pet Shop Boys have often commented on the slipperiness of gender and sexuality in the personae they create. See, for example, Simon Watney, "How to Have Sex in an Epidemic,"

Art-forum, November 1993, 8–9. In an article on the Doors' "L.A. Woman" and John Rechy's novel of the gay underground, *City of Night*, Ortíz claims that Morrison is singing about women who are actually men. Ricardo L. Ortíz, "L.A. Woman: Jim Morrison with John Rechy," *Literature and Psychology* 44, no. 3 (1988): 41–78.

4. "In the Pet Shop Boys' 1991 performances hardly a word was said to the audience until the penultimate song, and the visualization of the songs, rather than being based on video clips, introduced new imagery. Thus the PSB underscored the task of decoding visual imagery in live performance and asked us to take the songs, rather than their narrators, as the main focus of the show, just as in opera or modern dance we are expected to concentrate on the diegetic space rather than the performers or the composer. As in film, television, and theater, this performance seemed to demand that we inhabit the fictional world of the text, as opposed to the conventions of pop, where we are supposed to inhabit the emotions of the performers." Andrew Goodwin, *Dancing in the Distraction Factory: Music Television and Popular Culture* (Minneapolis: University of Minnesota Press, 1992), 102.

Permissions

"Hallo Spaceboy," written by David Bowie and Brian Eno, copyright 1995 by Upala Music, Inc., and Tintoretto Music/RZO Music, Inc. All rights reserved. Lyrics reprinted with permission by Tintoretto Music/RZO Music, Inc.

"China Girl," written by Iggy Pop and David Bowie, copyright 1977 James Osterberg Music (BMI). Administered by BUG EMI/Music Publishing/Jones Music America. All rights reserved. Lyrics reprinted with permission by Tintoretto Music/RZO Music, Inc.

"John, I'm Only Dancing," words by David Bowie, music by David Bowie and Brian Eno, copyright 1972 (renewed 2000) EMI Music Publishing Ltd., Tintoretto Music, and Moth Music. All rights for EMI Music Publishing Ltd. controlled and administered by Screen Gems–EMI Music, Inc. All rights for Tintoretto Music administered by RZO Music. All rights for Moth Music administered by Chrysalis Songs. All rights reserved. International copyright secured. Lyrics used by permission and courtesy of RZO Music, Inc.

"Boys Keep Swinging," words by David Bowie, music by David Bowie and Brian Eno, copyright 1979 EMI Music Publishing Ltd., Tintoretto Music, and BMG Music Publishing Ltd. All rights for EMI Music

Index

xvii, 149n21, 150n22, 176n1;
"Symphony in Yellow," 15; and
synesthesia, 13–14; and *Teleny*,
29–36, 38–47, 50, 163n21,
164n22; "The Truth of Masks,"
17, 184n15
Williams, Carolyn, 148n9
Williams, Tennessee, 86, 178n22,
181n52
Willis, Paul, 115
Wittig, Monique, 54, 59
Wolf, Reva, 175n52, 180n43

Wolfe, Tom, 176n5
Woman's World, The, 63

Yamamoto, Kansai, 111
Yeats, William Butler, xiv, 66–67;
Autobiographies, xiv, xvi;
*The Autobiography of William
Butler Yeats*, 159n67

Zola, Émile, 33, 148n12, 150n21,
176n5

Shelton Waldrep is associate professor of English at the University of Southern Maine. He is coauthor (with Jane Kuenz and Susan Willis) of *Inside the Mouse: Work and Play at Disney World* and editor of *The Seventies: The Age of Glitter in Popular Culture*.

	DATE DUE		